Six Sisters' STUFF

Six Sisters' STUFF

FAMILY RECIPES, FUN CRAFTS, AND SO MUCH MORE!

SHADOW
MOUNTAIN

TO OUR PARENTS
FOR ALWAYS SUPPORTING US

All photographs courtesy SixSistersStuff.com, except for photographs on pages 33, 70, 73, 104, 138, courtesy of Shutterstock.

Visit us at ShadowMountain.com

Library of Congress Cataloging-in-Publication Data

Six sisters' stuff : family recipes, fun crafts, and so much more.
   pages cm
  Includes index.
  Summary: Popular recipes and crafts from the blog Six sisters' stuff.
  ISBN 978-1-60907-324-4 (paperbound)
  1. Handicraft.
  TX714.S5858 2013
  641.5–dc23   2012047357

Printed in the United States of America
Worzalla Publishing Co., Stevens Point, WI

10 9 8 7 6 5 4 3 2 1

LINDA SEMINAR

CONTENTS

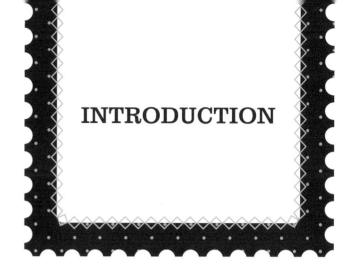

INTRODUCTION

We are six sisters—really! We don't have any brothers, and growing up, our parents taught us the importance of spending time together as a family. We knew we would sit down together every night for dinner and tell each other about our days. Even though, as sisters, we didn't always get along when we were young, our mom constantly reminded us that one day, we would become each other's best friends—and she was right. No matter the point we are at in our lives or what we have going on, our bond of sisterhood keeps us together.

Our love of recipes, crafts, and family traditions led us to start our blog *Six Sisters' Stuff*. It became our way to continue to share our ideas with each other even while our lives were heading in separate directions. We posted our favorite family-friendly recipes, quick crafts, and DIY projects. As our blog grew in size, scope, and popularity, we started receiving daily requests from other people asking us if we would consider compiling our recipes into a cookbook.

We wanted to create a collection of simple recipes, crafts, and ideas that could help busy parents and families spend less time cooking in the kitchen and more time creating lasting memories together. Our recipes use common ingredients that you probably already have in your pantry, and our do-it-yourself projects can beautify your home with little money or effort. We hope you enjoy our "stuff," and we welcome you to the sisterhood!

Black Bean Taco Soup

This is one of my family's favorite meals; we eat it year-round! Not only is it yummy, it is so easy—just pour all the ingredients in, mix together, and simmer for about 25 minutes. It's totally fail-proof. It makes an easy freezer meal, too. After cooking, let the soup cool, and then pour into a resealable gallon-sized plastic bag or other freezer container. When you are ready to eat the soup, let it thaw in the fridge for 24 hours, then reheat on the stove or in the microwave.—Kristen

- 1 pound ground beef (or ground turkey)
- 1 medium onion, chopped
- 1 (1.5-ounce) package mild taco seasoning mix
- 1 (16-ounce) can corn, undrained
- 1 (16-ounce) can black beans, drained and rinsed (you could also use kidney beans or pinto beans)
- 1 (14-ounce) can stewed tomatoes
- 1 (14-ounce) can diced tomatoes
- 1 (8-ounce) can tomato sauce
- 1 (4-ounce) can diced green chilies

    Tortilla chips

    Optional taco toppings: cheese, sour cream, avocado, etc.

Brown meat and onion. Drain. Stir in taco seasoning, corn, black beans, tomatoes, tomato sauce, and green chilies. Simmer on low heat for 20 to 30 minutes. Serve with tortilla chips and your favorite toppings.

Makes 6 to 8 servings.

Cheesy Vegetable Soup

On a cold winter day, a warm bowl of soup really hits the spot and this is one of our family's favorites. We called this "Cheese Soup" growing up, but it's as loaded with veggies as it is cheese! This recipe can easily be doubled so you can freeze half for another night. When you finish making it, let the soup cool, pour it into a gallon-sized resealable plastic bag or other freezer container, and store in the freezer. When you want to eat it, thaw the soup in the fridge and reheat it on the stovetop until warm.

2   cubes chicken or beef bouillon

1   cup water

1   cup diced celery

2   cups diced potatoes

1   cup diced carrots

1   (10-ounce) package frozen mixed vegetables (such as a broccoli, carrot, and cauliflower combo)

1   (10.5-ounce) can condensed cream of chicken soup

1½ cups milk

1   (16-ounce) block Velveeta cheese, cubed

Place bouillon, water, celery, potatoes, and carrots in a large pot and bring to a boil. Simmer until bouillon cubes have dissolved. Add frozen veggies and reduce heat to low. Cover and let simmer 30 to 40 minutes (add more water if liquid begins to evaporate).

Stir in cream of chicken soup, milk, and Velveeta cheese. Stir constantly until cheese is melted. Serve in bread bowls or with warm rolls.

Makes 6 servings.

WOODEN SNOWMAN

This little snowman is super easy to make. Purchase a 4x4 at a hardware store and ask a sales associate to cut it into 3 pieces of the following lengths: 4 inches, 6 inches, 8 inches, and then cut a small triangle from the end of the remaining 4x4. Alternatively, find a piece of scrap wood at home and use a handsaw to cut the pieces.

SUPPLIES

- **wood (see above)**
- **white paint**
- **black paint**
- **orange paint**
- **3 black buttons**
- **wood glue**
- **sandpaper**

INSTRUCTIONS

1. **Paint blocks.** Paint the 3 wooden blocks white. Once dry, sand the edges for a rustic look.

2. **Paint nose.** Paint the triangle orange. If desired, sand the edges once it is dry.

3. **Glue buttons.** Glue the three buttons down the front of your blocks. Glue the nose to the middle of the smallest wood block. To make the eyes, dip an unsharpened pencil into black paint and and make 2 dots right above the nose.

4. **Assemble snowman.** Stack the blocks to complete the snowman.

Philly Cheesesteak Sloppy Joes

Philly Cheesesteak sandwiches are one of our favorites, and when you combine them with the ease of sloppy joes, you have a yummy meal your entire family will love.

1 pound ground beef or sliced sirloin

1 onion, chopped

1 green pepper, chopped

1 (10-ounce) package fresh sliced mushrooms

¼ cup steak sauce

1 cup beef broth

Salt and pepper

Provolone cheese, sliced

6 to 8 hoagie buns or hard rolls

Turn oven to broil. In a large skillet over medium-high heat, brown the ground beef or sliced sirloin 5 to 6 minutes. Add onion, green pepper, and mushrooms, and cook another 3 to 4 minutes. Stir in steak sauce and beef broth. Season with salt and pepper. Bring to a simmer, and cook about 2 minutes.

Split rolls open, place one slice of cheese on one side of each roll and toast under broiler. Keep your eye on them so they don't burn. Place a scoopful of meat on the bottom half of the bun, drizzle with additional steak sauce, and place the cheesy half of the bun on top.

Makes 6 to 8 sandwiches.

The Best Hamburger Recipe (and Secret Sauce)

These burgers are moist, flavorful, and delicious, but it is the secret sauce that takes these hamburgers from ordinary to extraordinary! Don't be afraid of the 85-percent lean ground beef; you need a fattier meat to make a juicier burger.

1 pound 85-percent lean ground beef	Freshly ground black pepper to taste
½ cup shredded Monterey Jack cheese	Onion powder to taste
¼ cup barbecue sauce	6 sesame seed buns
Seasoned salt to taste	1 recipe Secret Sauce

Combine ground beef, cheese, barbecue sauce, and seasonings. Shape mixture into patties that are about 1 inch thick. You can get 5 to 6 patties with the mixture.

Heat grill until it is very hot. Reduce heat to medium-high and place the patties on the grill. Cook one side of the patty for 4 to 6 minutes, making sure it doesn't burn. Flip the patties over and cook until done, about 2 to 3 minutes. Serve on buns with a generous topping of Secret Sauce, as well as tomatoes, avocado, lettuce, or other favorite burger toppings.

Makes 5 to 6 burgers.

SECRET SAUCE

¾ cup mayonnaise	2 tablespoons Worcestershire sauce
¼ cup ketchup	¼ teaspoon seasoned salt
¼ cup sweet relish	

Combine all ingredients in a small bowl and use to top burgers. Leftovers can be stored in the refrigerator 3 to 4 days.

Baked Ziti

I participate in a freezer-meal group in my neighborhood. Once a month each person prepares five meals of the same freezer meal. We then get together and swap meals, sending each of us home with five different meals that are ready to eat in a matter of minutes! This recipe is one of my favorites for freezing.—Camille

1 pound ziti noodles, uncooked (or any pasta noodle)	¼ teaspoon garlic powder or minced garlic
1 onion, chopped	2 (26-ounce) jars spaghetti sauce
1 pound lean ground beef	8 slices provolone cheese
Salt	1½ cups sour cream
Pepper	6 ounces mozzarella cheese, shredded
	2 tablespoons grated Parmesan cheese

Preheat oven to 350 degrees F. Spray two 8x8-inch pans with nonstick cooking spray.

Bring a large pot of lightly salted water to a boil. Add ziti and cook until al dente, about 7 to 8 minutes; drain.

In a large skillet, brown onion and ground beef over medium heat. Season with salt, pepper, and garlic to taste. Add spaghetti sauce and simmer 15 minutes.

Layer as follows in each prepared pan: ¼ of the cooked ziti, about 1½ cups of sauce, 4 slices of provolone cheese, ¾ cup sour cream, ¼ of the cooked ziti, ¼ of the mozzarella cheese, and another 1½ cups of sauce.

Top with grated Parmesan cheese and remaining mozzarella cheese. Bake, covered, for 30 minutes or until cheeses are melted. Ingredients fill the 8x8-inch pans to the top, so I cook mine on a large cookie sheet—just in case they bubble over.

You can eat one for dinner now and freeze the other for dinner another day!

Makes 10 to 12 servings.

20-Minute Skillet Lasagna

Sometimes you just need something you can put together in a matter of minutes. This skillet lasagna recipe is so fast and easy, you can whip up dinner faster than you can watch one episode of *Dora the Explorer*.

1 pound lean ground beef	½ teaspoon garlic powder
1 (12-ounce) package bow tie noodles	1 teaspoon Italian seasoning (or more, according to taste)
1 (26-ounce) jar spaghetti sauce	½ cup shredded mozzarella cheese
1 tablespoon olive oil	½ cup sour cream
1 teaspoon salt	

Brown ground beef in a small pan over medium heat. Meanwhile, cook noodles according to package directions. After noodles are cooked, drain off water and drizzle noodles with olive oil. Mix in spaghetti sauce. Add browned beef, seasonings, cheese, and sour cream. Fold together and allow it all to combine and heat through over low heat for about 5 minutes, or until cheese is melted. Serve with a simple green salad and loaf of French bread to complete your meal.

Makes 6 servings.

PALLET BOOKSHELVES

Kids love books, but parents hate having books scattered all over the place. To remedy this, check out local grocery stores for discarded pallets. Once you find one that's in good shape, bring it home, tear it apart, use some primer and paint to fix it up, and make your own inexpensive bookshelves.

SUPPLIES

- pallet
- handsaw
- sandpaper or an electric sander
- spray primer (Kilz Spray Primer works best)
- spray paint, any color
- Hercules Hooks
- swivel hangers

INSTRUCTIONS

1. **Cut up pallet.** Use a handsaw to make two cuts in your pallet, as shown in the image on the following page. Make sure to cut as straight as possible.

2. **Pry pallet apart.** Pry off the boards in the middle of the pallet. Attach two of the boards removed from the pallet to the bottom of each shelf using two nails on each end.

3. **Sand shelves.** Sand down your shelves and the boards you will be nailing across the bottom. If you use an electric sander, this task can take under 30 minutes.

4. **Prime shelves.** Use spray primer to prime your shelves. Be sure to have some brushes handy in case the primer drips.

5. **Paint shelves.** Spray 2 to 3 coats of paint over shelves. Alternatively, you can use a brush and a good, old-fashioned can of paint.

6. **Sand down edges.** This step is optional. If you want a rustic look, sand down the edges by hand.

7. **Hang shelves.** Attach 3 swivel hangers, evenly spaced, to the back of each shelf. Hold shelves up against the wall and mark the locations where swivel hangers will meet the wall. Hammer a Hercules Hook into each location. (The great thing about these hooks is that you can hang things directly into the wall without being in a stud. Each hook holds up to 150 pounds, so this is definitely strong enough to hold books.) Hang shelves.

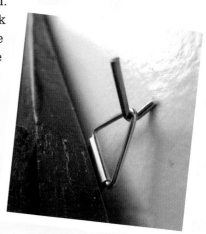

Sausage and Egg Breakfast Casserole

This casserole can be easily prepared the night before and put in the fridge overnight. Reheat it in the oven the next morning for a delicious breakfast.

10 eggs, lightly beaten

3 cups milk

1 teaspoon salt

1 loaf crusty French bread, cubed or torn into small pieces, divided

1 green pepper, diced, divided

1 red pepper, diced, divided

½ cup diced onion, divided

2 cups Colby Jack or cheddar cheese, divided

½ pound sausage, cooked and crumbled, divided

½ teaspoon black pepper

Preheat oven to 325 degrees F. Coat a 9x13-inch glass baking pan with nonstick cooking spray. Combine eggs, milk, and salt in a bowl; set aside. Distribute half of the bread evenly in the prepared pan. Sprinkle over the bread half of each of the following ingredients: green pepper, red pepper, onion, cheese, and sausage. Repeat the layering again, beginning with bread. Sprinkle black pepper on top. Pour the egg mixture over the casserole and bake 60 minutes. Refrigerate any leftovers.

Makes 8 to 10 servings.

Cheesy Enchilada Casserole

Every Sunday I plan out my menu for the week, and I usually don't realize until I get to the grocery store the next day that I have planned Mexican dishes for 3 or more of the 7 meals for the week. I love Mexican food. I just can't get enough! My husband is learning to love it almost as much as I do, and he definitely liked this one. So does the toddler!—Elyse

1   pound 90-percent lean ground beef

1   large onion, chopped

2½ cups salsa

1   (15-ounce) can black beans or red kidney beans, rinsed and drained

¼   cup reduced-fat Italian salad dressing

½   cup reduced-fat sour cream

1   (15-ounce) can corn, drained, or 1¼ cups frozen corn (optional)

2   tablespoons reduced-sodium taco seasoning

¼   teaspoon ground cumin

2   cups grated, reduced-fat Mexican cheese blend, divided

6   (8-inch) flour or corn tortillas, depending on taste

1   cup shredded lettuce

1   medium tomato, chopped

¼   cup minced fresh cilantro

    Olives, sliced

Preheat oven to 400 degrees F.

In a large skillet, cook beef and onion over medium heat until meat is no longer pink; drain. Stir in salsa, beans, dressing, sour cream, taco seasoning, corn, and cumin. Spoon a layer of meat mixture into a 2-quart baking dish. Sprinkle with about ½ cup grated cheese. Place 1 or 2 tortillas on top of meat mixture. Layer with half of the remaining meat mixture and cheese. Repeat. The final layer should be a healthy handful of cheese. Coat a piece of foil with nonstick cooking spray, cover casserole dish, and bake 25 minutes, or until hot and bubbly.

Cool for 5 minutes before topping with lettuce, tomato, cilantro, and olives.

Makes 6 to 8 servings.

Easy Chicken Spaghetti

This meal is seriously so simple to throw together and it's incredibly versatile—you can pretty much throw in whatever vegetables you have on hand and it always turns out delicious! I have used zucchini, sautéed mushrooms, pimentos, and green chilies (basically anything goes!). This is a meal the entire family will always eat.

1 (16-ounce) package uncooked spaghetti noodles

2 cups cooked, chopped chicken

2 (10.75-ounce) cans 98-percent fat-free cream of chicken or cream of mushroom soup

¼ cup diced onion

¼ cup diced green pepper

1 (14.5-ounce) can diced tomatoes, drained

3 cups grated cheddar cheese, divided

1 teaspoon seasoned salt

Cayenne pepper (optional)

1 (14.5-ounce) can chicken broth

Preheat oven to 350 degrees F. Coat a 9x13-inch glass pan with nonstick cooking spray.

Break spaghetti noodles into 2- to 3-inch pieces and cook according to package directions. Place cooked noodles into a large bowl. Add chicken and toss together. Add cream of chicken soup, onion, green pepper, tomatoes, 2 cups cheese, seasoned salt, and a dash of cayenne pepper. Mix all together. Slowly add about 1 cup chicken broth. Stir it in and add a little bit more, but be careful not to let mixture become soupy.

Pour spaghetti mixture into pan and top with remaining cheese. Bake 30 to 35 minutes or until hot and bubbly.

Makes 8 servings.

Baked Chicken Fajitas

These fajitas not only taste amazing and are full of flavor, but they are loaded with delicious vegetables! The best part of this dish is being able to throw everything into one pan and toss it in the oven—it doesn't get any easier than that.

1 pound boneless, skinless chicken breasts, cut into strips	3 teaspoons chili powder
1 (15-ounce) can diced tomatoes	2 teaspoons cumin
1 (7-ounce) can diced green chilies	½ teaspoon garlic powder
1 large bell pepper, seeded and sliced	½ teaspoon dried oregano
1 medium onion, sliced	¼ teaspoon salt
2 tablespoons vegetable oil	12 flour tortillas, warmed
	Sliced avocados

Preheat oven to 400 degrees F. Grease a 9x13-inch baking dish.

Mix together chicken, tomatoes, chilies, pepper, and onion in the dish. In a small bowl, combine oil and spices. Drizzle spice mixture over chicken and toss to coat. Bake, uncovered, 20 to 25 minutes, or until chicken is cooked through and vegetables are tender. Serve with warmed tortillas and sliced avocados.

Makes 4 to 6 servings.

Baked Chicken Bacon Ranch Taquitos

I have to be honest—there are a lot of recipe-fails at my house. Most of them happen when I try to invent my own recipe. My poor husband dreads those experimental meals. But every once in a while something wonderful comes of it, and these little taquitos fall into that "wonderful" category! They are quick and easy to throw together. You can prepare the filling early in the day and even roll the taquitos, keep them in the fridge, and then pop them in the oven when you are ready to eat dinner. Looking for a yummy freezer meal? You can easily prep these and then freeze them. They even make great lunches—just pull the number you need out of the freezer and bake!—Camille

1 (8-ounce) package cream cheese, softened	3 to 4 tablespoons chopped green onion
4 cups cooked, shredded chicken	1 (1-ounce) packet dry ranch dressing mix
12 slices bacon, cooked and crumbled	20 (6-inch) flour tortillas
2 cups shredded Monterey Jack cheese	Salt

Preheat oven to 425 degrees F. Cover a large baking sheet with aluminum foil and coat lightly with nonstick cooking spray.

Mix together cream cheese, chicken, bacon, shredded cheese, and green onions. Add in about ½ of the dry ranch dressing mix and taste. Add more for stronger ranch flavor. Mix well. Spoon 2 to 3 tablespoons of the chicken mixture into a flour tortilla and roll it up. Place taquito seam-side down on the baking sheet. Repeat about 20 times. Once finished, spray the tops of the taquitos with nonstick cooking spray (or lightly brush olive oil on them) and sprinkle with salt. (I like to use sea salt.)

Place pan in oven and bake 10 to 15 minutes or until edges and tops are golden. Let cool 2 to 3 minutes. Serve with ranch dressing or bleu cheese dressing for dipping. (My husband also likes to dip them in Salsa Ranch—just mix equal parts salsa and ranch dressing together.)

Makes 16 taquitos.

Barbecue Chicken Calzones

I had some extra biscuits lying around one day and thought I would put them to good use. I found a few different calzone recipes online and combined them to make this. We thought they were pretty good, and if my picky toddler will eat something, it is definitely a keeper!—Elyse

6 slices bacon

1 tablespoon olive oil

½ small onion, chopped

3 cups cooked, shredded chicken

1 (20-ounce) bottle barbecue sauce, divided

1 can refrigerated biscuits

1 cup shredded mozzarella cheese

2 tablespoons chopped fresh cilantro (optional)

Preheat oven to 400 degrees F.

Cook bacon in a large skillet over medium-high heat until crisp. Remove from pan and drain on paper towels; crumble. Drain bacon fat from pan (or use bacon fat instead of the oil). Warm olive oil over medium heat; add onion and shredded chicken and sauté until onion is tender. Stir in ½ cup barbecue sauce, and remove from the heat. Mix in cooked bacon.

Flatten out biscuit dough onto a greased cookie sheet. Press to an even thickness. Spread a small amount of barbecue sauce on each biscuit (about 1 teaspoon). Divide the chicken mixture between the biscuits, spreading on only half of each piece to within ½ inch of the edge. Sprinkle cheese and cilantro over the top. Fold each biscuit in half and press the edges together with a fork to seal.

Bake 12 to 15 minutes or until browned to your liking. Cool for a few minutes. These can be served with additional barbecue sauce.

Makes 4 to 6 servings.

Red Potatoes and Ham Casserole

I had seen a recipe similar to this for the slow cooker; but the first time I made it, I forgot to start it in the morning and had only 35 minutes before dinnertime. I decided to improvise since I was short on time, and the final outcome was delicious!—Camille

6 to 8   red potatoes

2 cups diced, cooked ham

1 (10.75-ounce) can cream of potato soup

1   envelope dry ranch salad dressing mix

1   (8-ounce) package cream cheese, softened

Preheat oven to 350 degrees F. Chop potatoes into large cubes and place in a 4-quart pot. Cover with water, place over high heat, and boil until softened. Mix potatoes with ham and place in a 9x13-inch baking dish. In a small bowl, beat together soup, salad dressing mix, and cream cheese. Stir into potatoes and ham. Cover and cook for 30 to 35 minutes.

Makes 6 servings.

Mom's Pork Chop Marinade

Our mom gave me this recipe years ago, and it has become a family favorite! I usually have all the ingredients on hand, so it is very easy to assemble. I had never had such a delicious and tender grilled pork chop before I tried this recipe!—Camille

½ cup soy sauce

¼ cup chili sauce

¼ cup honey

2 tablespoons vegetable oil

2 tablespoons chopped green onion

1 teaspoon curry powder

4 to 6 boneless pork chops

Combine all ingredients except pork chops in a medium bowl. Pour marinade into a resealable gallon-sized plastic bag, add pork chops, and seal. Place the bag in a clean bowl and marinate in the fridge 6 to 8 hours or overnight. Grill and enjoy!

Makes 4 to 6 servings.

Grilled Island Chicken Kebabs

Shish kebabs were always one of our favorite meals growing up. Who doesn't love eating food from a stick? Even veggies are more fun when skewered.

⬦⬦⬦

⅓ cup vegetable oil

¼ cup fresh or bottled lemon juice

2 tablespoons soy sauce

1 clove garlic, finely minced

½ teaspoon dried oregano

¼ teaspoon salt

¼ teaspoon freshly ground black pepper

2 to 4 chicken breasts, cut into large, bite-sized chunks

1 large red onion, cut into large chunks

1 large green pepper, cut into large chunks

1 pineapple, cut into large chunks

Combine vegetable oil, lemon juice, soy sauce, garlic, oregano, salt, and pepper in a resealable gallon-sized plastic bag. Place chicken in bag and make sure all pieces are covered. Marinate chicken in the refrigerator for at least 3 hours, and up to 12 hours.

If using wooden skewers, let your skewers soak in water for at least 30 minutes before grilling (to prevent burning). Thread chicken, onion, pepper, and pineapple on your sticks until you run out of ingredients. Heat grill to medium heat. Place skewers on grill and cook 7 to 8 minutes per side or until chicken is no longer pink in the middle and registers 160 degrees F. on a meat thermometer.

Remove from grill and serve.

Makes 4 servings.

SPRING CLEANING CHECKLIST

If you feel overwhelmed by the idea of spring cleaning, consider breaking it down room by room and tackling a new room every week. These lists do just that and give you an idea of what to accomplish in each room.

Foyer

Dust light fixtures.

Wash walls and trim.

Wash doors, knobs, and switch plates.

Wash bench or other furnishings. Launder bench cushion, if applicable.

Empty out coat closet. Wash walls and floor. Sort items as you return them to the closet. Store out-of-season items and donate unneeded items.

Clean or replace entry mat.

Sweep and scrub floors.

Bedrooms

Dust furniture.

For each drawer: remove items, wash drawer, place items you need back neatly; donate items you no longer need.

Remove everything from closets. Wash closet walls if necessary. Sweep or vacuum closet floor. Put everything back neatly. Donate items you no longer need. Do not store things on closet floor.

Move bed. Sort and put away anything that was under bed. Sweep or vacuum under bed.

Flip or rotate mattress. Vacuum both sides.

Launder bedding and curtains. Wash pillows and duvet in hot water. Air out mattress pad.

Dust light fixtures.

Clean lampshades.

Wash windows and windowsills. Take out and wash window screens.

Wash switch plates.

Wash walls and trim.

Wash mirrors and dust art.

Wash doors and doorknobs.

Wash floor registers and other vent covers.

Sweep and wash floor or vacuum.

Bathrooms

Open windows.

Empty all cabinets and vanity. Wash inside, replace items neatly. Discard expired medications and cosmetics.

Wash outside of cabinets and vanities.

Clean tub. Wax if necessary. Clean drain.

Clean toilet, inside and out. Remove seat and clean around seat bolts.

Clean sink and drain.

Shine faucets.

Clean mirror and frame.

Dust light fixtures.

Wash windows and windowsills. Take out and wash window screens.

Wash switch plates.

Wash walls and trim.

Wash doors and doorknobs.

Wash floor registers and other vent covers.

Sweep and wash floors.

Reseal grout lines.

Kitchen

Open windows.

Remove and clean window coverings.

For each cabinet or drawer: Remove items, wipe out drawer, place items back neatly. Donate unneeded items.

Wash and sanitize cutting boards.

Sharpen knives.

Wash cabinet doors and knobs.

Clean and organize pantry. Check food expiration dates.

Clean oven.

Clean stove top. Remove elements and drip bowls, if applicable; wash and put back.

Clean and organize fridge and freezer. Defrost freezer, if necessary. Check food expiration dates.

Clean under fridge and stove.

Vacuum refrigerator coils.

Clean microwave.

Clean crumbs out of toaster.

Clean and descale kettle.

Wipe down any other counter appliances.

Wash counters and back splash.

Wash and shine sink. Shine faucet. Clean drain.

Dust light fixtures.

Wash windows and windowsills. Remove window screens and wash.

Wash switch plates.

Wash walls and trim.

Wash doors and doorknobs.

Wash floor registers and other vent covers.

Sweep and wash floor.

Reseal grout lines, if applicable.

Dining Room

Open windows.

Wash curtains.

Wipe down table and chairs.

Wipe down or dust other furnishings.

Clean chair pads, if applicable.

Polish table, if necessary.

Dust any displayed china or serving dishes.

Launder table linens.

Shine silverware.

Dust art.

Wash windows and windowsills. Take out and wash window screens.

Wash switch plates.

Wash walls and trim.

Wash doors and doorknobs.

Wash floor registers and other vent covers.

Clean floors.

Living Room/Family Room/Playroom

Open windows.

Vacuum sofas.

Spot clean sofas, if applicable.

Launder throw pillows and blankets.

Dust shelves, furniture, and decor.

Clean lamps and lampshades.

Wash windows and windowsills.

Take out and wash window screens.

Clean television screen.

Carefully dust electronics.

Tidy wires to electronics, such as television, computer, stereo systems, etc. Tuck nicely out of sight. Label them, if practical.

Sort through music and DVD collections. Donate things that no longer suit your family's interests. Organize what is left in an attractive manner.

Sort books and magazines. Donate or recycle ones that no longer suit your family's interests.

Wash hard plastic children's toys with warm soapy water. Rinse and dry. Launder stuffed toys. Donate or store toys your children have outgrown.

Wash switch plates.

Wash walls and trim.

Wash doors and knobs.

Wash floor registers and other vent covers.

Clean floors.

Laundry Room

Open windows.

Wash windows and windowsills.

Take out and wash window screens.

Wash cabinet doors.

Wash inside cabinets.

Wash laundry sink. Shine faucet. Clean drains.

Wash outside of washer and dryer.

Wash inside of washing machine.

Wash lint trap.

Wash switch plates.

Wash walls and trim.

Wash doors and doorknobs.

Wash floor registers and other vent covers.

Sweep and wash floors.

Reseal grout lines, if applicable.

Stairwells

Sweep or vacuum stairs.

Spot-clean walls.

Wipe down handrail.

Dust art and light fixtures.

Outdoors

Sweep porches and walkway.

Wash thresholds.

Wash exterior doors. Give front door a fresh coat of paint, if necessary.

Clean or replace welcome mat.

Wash siding.

Other

Clean blades of ceiling fans.

Dust blinds, if applicable.

Sort through and organize family photographs (digitally or into albums).

Sort through paperwork and discard unneeded files. Date and file important documents in an orderly manner.

Sort and clean any extra zones, such as linen closets, utility closets, and office spaces.

Baked Sweet and Sour Chicken

We think this sweet and sour chicken is good enough to be take-out!

3 to 4 boneless, skinless, chicken breasts
Salt and pepper to taste
1½ cups cornstarch
3 eggs, beaten
¼ cup canola oil
1 cup sugar

4 tablespoons ketchup
¼ cup white vinegar
¼ cup apple cider vinegar
1 tablespoon soy sauce
1 teaspoon garlic salt

Preheat oven to 325 degrees F. Rinse chicken breasts in water and then cut into bite-sized pieces. Season with salt and pepper to taste. Place cornstarch in a shallow dish. Place beaten eggs in a separate shallow dish. Heat oil in a large skillet over medium-high heat. Dredge chicken in beaten eggs and then in cornstarch. Add to hot oil and cook until browned on both sides, 3 to 4 minutes. Place the chicken in a 9x13-inch greased baking dish. Whisk together sugar, ketchup, vinegar, soy sauce, and garlic salt in a bowl and then pour evenly over the chicken. Bake for one hour, turning the chicken every 15 minutes.

Makes 4 servings.

Chicken and Cream Cheese Roll-Ups with Chicken Gravy

Our mom has been making these for as long as we can remember, and they have always been a family favorite. Our kids love these because they are easy to eat with their hands. There are lots of variations of this recipe out there, but we think this one is the best.

4   boneless, skinless chicken breasts, cooked and shredded

1   (8-ounce) package cream cheese, softened

1 to 2   tablespoons chopped onion, according to taste

1   (4-ounce) can mushrooms, or ½ cup chopped fresh mushrooms

2   tablespoons butter, melted

2   cans refrigerated crescent rolls (Pillsbury rolls work best)

Preheat oven to 350 degrees F.

Combine cooked chicken, cream cheese, onions, mushrooms, and butter in a medium bowl; set aside.

Roll out the crescents. Place a heaping spoonful of chicken mixture on wide-end of each crescent and roll it up. Place crescents on large baking sheet or jelly roll pan. Bake 12 to 14 minutes, or until rolls are golden brown. Serve with chicken gravy if desired.

Makes 6 servings.

CHICKEN GRAVY

1   (10.75-ounce) can cream of chicken soup

¼   cup sour cream

1 to 2   tablespoons milk

Mix all ingredients in a saucepan and warm through. Serve with rolls.

Parmesan Sesame Chicken Strips

These are a grown-up version of chicken nuggets you can share with the kids. They taste delicious dipped in homemade honey mustard sauce, or you can use ketchup if you prefer.

35 Ritz crackers (butter flavor)	¼ cup sesame seeds
1 cup mayonnaise (regular or light)	¼ cup grated Parmesan cheese
2 teaspoons dried minced onion	4 boneless, skinless chicken breasts
2 teaspoons ground mustard	Homemade Honey Mustard Dipping Sauce

Preheat oven to 425 degrees F. Cover a large baking sheet with aluminum foil and lightly coat with nonstick cooking spray.

Place crackers in a resealable gallon-sized plastic bag and crush them with a rolling pin until they are fine crumbs. In a bowl, combine mayonnaise, onion, and mustard. In a second bowl, combine crushed crackers, sesame seeds, and Parmesan cheese. Cut chicken lengthwise into quarter-inch strips. Dip strips into mayonnaise mixture, and then into crumb mixture. Place chicken on foil-covered baking sheet. Bake 15 to 18 minutes. Serve with honey mustard dipping sauce (or ketchup!).

Makes 4 to 6 servings.

HOMEMADE HONEY MUSTARD DIPPING SAUCE

½ cup light or regular mayonnaise	3 tablespoons honey
2 tablespoons yellow mustard	½ tablespoon lemon juice
1 tablespoon Dijon mustard	

Combine all ingredients and enjoy!

Grilled 7-Up Chicken

Our mom has been making this chicken for as long as we can remember, and everyone always asks for the recipe when she does. The chicken has amazing flavor and is incredibly moist. The marinade tastes awesome with pork too!

½ cup soy sauce

½ teaspoon horseradish

1 (12-ounce) can lemon-lime soda (not diet)

¼ cup vegetable oil

4 to 6 boneless, skinless chicken breasts

Combine all ingredients except chicken in a medium bowl. Pour marinade into a resealable gallon-sized plastic bag. Add chicken breasts and seal. Place the bag in a clean bowl and marinate in the refrigerator for 30 minutes or up to overnight. Heat grill. Grill chicken breasts on one side 5 to 6 minutes. Turn and grill an additional 4 to 5 minutes, being careful not to overcook. Test breasts with a meat thermometer. The chicken is completely cooked through when a meat thermometer registers 155 degrees F.

Makes 4 to 6 servings.

Aussie Chicken and Honey Mustard Sauce

If you are looking to spice up plain ol' chicken breasts, this recipe is a winner!

◇◇

4 boneless, skinless chicken breasts, pounded to ½-inch thickness
Seasoning salt
6 slices bacon, cut in half
⅓ cup honey
¼ cup mustard

2 tablespoons mayonnaise
½ tablespoon dried onion flakes
1 tablespoon vegetable oil
1 cup fresh mushrooms, sliced
2 cups shredded Colby Jack cheese

Preheat oven to 350 degrees F. Rub the chicken breasts with seasoning salt. Cover and refrigerate for 30 minutes. Meanwhile, cook bacon in a large skillet until crisp; set aside.

In a small bowl, mix the honey, mustard, mayonnaise, and dried onion flakes; set aside. Heat oil in a large skillet over medium heat. Place chicken in the skillet and sauté 3 to 5 minutes per side, or until browned. Move chicken to an 7x11-inch or 9x9-inch pan. Spread the honey mustard over each breast, and then layer with mushrooms, bacon, and shredded cheese. Bake 20 to 25 minutes, or until cheese is melted and chicken is completely cooked through.

Makes 4 to 6 servings.

EASY MONSTER SOCK PUPPET

These darling monster sock puppets are perfect for entertaining the kiddos when outdoor play isn't an option. They are based on a tutorial from One of a Kind Gift Ideas (www.oneofakindgiftideas.blogspot.com). Make sure to find a sock long enough to cover your arm. The more colorful, the better!

SUPPLIES

- cardboard
- felt
- hot glue and glue gun
- long fuzzy sock
- pom-poms

INSTRUCTIONS

1. **Cut an oval for the mouth.** Cut a 4-inch long oval from the cardboard. Trace the cardboard oval twice on the felt and then cut out the corresponding felt ovals. Use hot glue to cover each side of the cardboard with a felt oval.

3. **Attach the mouth.** Roll the end of the sock under the edge of the cardboard and hot glue it to the felt-covered cardboard to create the mouth.

2. **Fold the mouth.** Cut the toe off the end of the sock, slide your arm through, and adjust the cardboard to work as a mouth by folding it in half.

4. **Decorate!** Glue on two pom-poms for eyes. Add smaller pom-poms to the center of the eyes, if desired. Cut triangles from the leftover felt and glue along the sock to make a razor back. Be creative!

Slow Cooker Steak Fajitas

I like to set out all our favorite toppings and let my kids pick what they want on their fajitas. It is the perfect way to get them to eat their vegetables.—Camille

1½ pounds sirloin steak	Soft tortillas
1 (4-ounce) can diced green chilies	Shredded cheese
1 envelope dry onion soup mix	Salsa
2 cups water	Guacamole
1 onion	Sour cream
1 green pepper	Canned corn, drained
1 tablespoon olive oil	Tomatoes

Cut sirloin steak into bite-sized pieces. Place steak in slow cooker with chilies, soup mix, and water, and cook on low 6 to 8 hours. Just before serving, slice onion and green pepper into strips and sauté in olive oil in a large skillet over medium heat. Remove meat from slow cooker using a slotted spoon and place meat, onion, green pepper, and whatever other toppings you like on tortillas.

Makes 6 servings.

Slow Cooker Pot Roast Sliders

This roast recipe is so moist that the meat practically falls apart when it is finished cooking. The aroma from all the flavors in the slow cooker will make your house smell amazing. You can eat the roast as is or shred it and eat it on sandwiches.

1 cup water

1 cup salsa

1 envelope onion soup mix

1 envelope Italian dressing mix

1 envelope au jus mix

1 (3- to 4-pound) beef roast

12 dinner rolls (or other slider rolls)

Sliced Swiss cheese (1 slice per slider)

Creamy Chipotle Sauce

Whisk together water, salsa, and seasoning packets. Place roast in slow cooker. Pour seasoning mixture over roast. Cook on low 8 to 10 hours, or high 4 to 5 hours. Shred beef. Cut each roll in half and place on a baking sheet. Place a slice of Swiss cheese on the bottom half of each roll. Place baking sheet in oven with broiler on low. Broil 1 to 2 minutes or until edges of the rolls are golden and cheese has melted. (Be sure to watch them closely so they don't burn!) Remove baking sheet from oven.

Place a spoonful of shredded beef on the bottom half of the toasted roll. Spread Creamy Chipotle sauce on the top half.

Makes 12 sliders.

CREAMY CHIPOTLE SAUCE

¼ cup sour cream

2 tablespoons chili sauce

2 teaspoons creamy horseradish sauce

Blend all ingredients in a small bowl.

Slow Cooker French Dip Sandwiches

These sandwiches are some of our favorites. They are incredibly easy to prepare and this recipe makes a lot, so it is the perfect dish to make when you have to feed a crowd.

1 (2- to 3-pound) beef or pork roast

2 (10.75-ounce) cans beef consommé

6 to 8 hoagie buns

Place roast in greased slow cooker. Pour consommé over the top of the roast. Cook on low 8 to 11 hours or on high 5 to 7 hours. Remove roast and save extra juice for dipping. With 2 forks, pull apart roast. (When it is done, it should pull apart easily.) Serve meat on buns and use extra juice as a dipping sauce for the sandwiches.

Makes 8 or more servings, depending on sandwich size.

Melt-in-Your-Mouth Slow Cooker Pot Roast

The combination of various sauces in this recipe turns pot roast into a mouth-watering feast with all the simplicity of a slow-cooker meal. This melt-in-your-mouth recipe is sure to become a family favorite.

1 (3- to 4-pound) beef chuck roast	¾ cup ketchup
1 (12-ounce) can Cola (not diet)	¾ packet dry onion soup mix
¾ cup dark brown sugar	4 to 5 new red potatoes, cut up
¾ cup Heinz chili sauce	1½ to 2 cups baby carrots

Combine all ingredients in a slow cooker. Cook on low 8 to 10 hours.

Makes 6 to 8 servings.

Slow Cooker Kalua Pork Roast

This pork is one of the easiest recipes to make, and it tastes absolutely amazing. You would never guess that so few ingredients could make such incredibly flavored meat! Serve it over rice and top with your favorite fresh vegetables for a tasty dinner. We love to make this for company because it feeds so many and gets rave reviews.

1 (2- to 4-pound) pork butt roast, fat trimmed	Chopped green peppers (optional)
1 tablespoon sea salt	Diced tomatoes (optional)
1 tablespoon liquid smoke flavoring	Chopped onions (optional)
3 to 4 cups cooked brown or white rice	Banana peppers (optional)
	Diced cucumbers (optional)

Pierce pork all over with a carving fork. Rub salt and liquid smoke over meat. Place roast in a slow cooker. Cover and cook on low 10 to 12 hours. Turn once about halfway through cooking time. Remove meat from slow cooker and shred with 2 forks (it will usually fall apart easily), adding drippings as needed to moisten.

Serve over rice, topped with your favorite veggies.

Makes 6 to 8 servings.

Slow Cooker Chile Verde Pork Tacos

This pork is very tender and full of flavor and requires very little work on your part! We love it in tacos, but it also tastes great on a salad, with tortilla chips, wrapped in a burrito, or even eaten as is!

1 (2- to 3-pound) pork roast	1 (16-ounce) jar green salsa
1 onion, minced	1 (4-ounce) can green chilies
3 cloves garlic, crushed	1 (14-ounce) can diced tomatoes
1 green pepper, finely chopped	1 teaspoon cumin
2 to 3 tomatillos, husked and chopped	Flour tortillas
1 jalapeño, seeded and chopped (optional)	Taco toppings, such as cheese, lettuce, avocado, tomato, sour cream

Spray a slow cooker with nonstick cooking spray. Place the roast in the slow cooker. Add onion, garlic, green pepper, tomatillos, jalapeño, salsa, chilies, diced tomatoes, and cumin. Cook on low 8 to 10 hours. Once finished, shred the roast with 2 forks. (It will literally fall apart.) Serve on flour tortillas for tacos and add desired toppings.

Makes 6 servings.

50 FUN DATE IDEAS

I never knew how difficult it would be to go on dates with my husband once we had a kid! We are lucky to get in a date every month or two. We decided that we would try to have a date night at least twice a month. Since it can be hard to find a sitter, I decided to compile a list of dates you can plan and do at home as well as out on the town, without breaking the bank. We've done a lot of these dates and have had a blast! I'm sure you will too!—Elyse

1. **Make your own fondue.** Use a fondue pot (or slow cooker) and dip fresh fruit, cake, cookies, marshmallows, and pretzels in melted chocolate. We like the delicious recipe at http://allrecipes.com/recipe/eagle-brand-chocolate-fondue/

2. **Make homemade pizzas together.**

3. **Fly kites.** You can usually find them at the dollar store.

4. **Try a new sport together.**

5. **Have a game night.** Pull out all of your board games for a friendly night of competition. Be sure to have some treats for the occasion, like our Gooey Almond and Coconut Chex Mix available at http://www.sixsistersstuff.com/2011/11/gooey-almond-and-coconut-chex-mix.html.

6. **Be a tourist in your own city.** Find out what tourist attractions are in your city and spend the night acting like tourists—don't forget to take lots of cheesy pictures!

7. **Go inline skating.** If the weather is bad, try an indoor skating rink.

8. **Explore.** Rent a four-wheeler, snowmobile, scooter, waver runner, or other vehicle and do a little exploring.

9. **Go to a thrift store.** Each person gets $5 to spend. See who ends up with the best item(s)!

10. **Have a picnic.** If the weather doesn't permit an outdoor picnic, lay out a blanket on the floor and eat in the living room.

11. **Go see a play.** Whether it's at your local community theater, high school, or a big-city play house, there is plenty of entertainment available in most areas.

12. **Stargazing.** Pack a blanket, pillows, and food (like our Ham and Swiss Poppy Seed Sandwiches), and go somewhere to see the stars. Do some research before you leave so you know which constellations to look for. You can find the recipe for the sandwiches at http://www.six

sistersstuff.com/2011/11
/ham-swiss-poppy-seed
-sandwich-sliders.html.

13. **Go to a park.** Swing on the swings, play Frisbee, or feed the ducks.

14. **Check out a local museum.** Local museums usually don't cost much to get in.

15. **Have a crazy dinner.** Each person gets $5 (or whatever amount you decide) to spend on any food item at the grocery store for dinner. Come home and prepare your meal. You might end up with something delightful!

16. **Make ice cream sundaes.** Head to the store and buy some vanilla ice cream and your favorite toppings. Relax and enjoy your tasty treat!

17. **Go to a local sporting event.** Luckily, sports are going on year-round. Grab some snacks and head out to the ball game!

18. **Go treasure hunting.** On a Saturday morning, head to the ATM and take out $10 to $20. Drive around to some local yard sales and see what you end up with.

19. **Go on a bike ride.** If you don't have a bike, check the classifieds for a great deal. You could even pack a lunch!

20. **Have a living-room campout.** Make a tent out of blankets, watch a movie, and sleep on an air mattress.

21. **Love Languages.** Take the 5 Love Languages Test available at http://www.5lovelanguages.com

to see how to improve your relationship. End the evening with some chocolate-dipped strawberries.

22. **Go for a swim.** Head to a local pool and relax in the hot tub.

23. **Have a coupon date.** Only eat or do activities for which you have coupons.

24. **Volunteer.** Sign up to volunteer at a soup kitchen, retirement home, or somewhere that could use a helping hand.

25. **Go to a local fair or carnival.** Be sure to bring some cash to play the games!

26. **Take a free factory tour.** You might be surprised what factories are around you!

27. **Visit the zoo.** If you don't live near a zoo, go somewhere to see your local wildlife.

28. **Take a drive.** Get out of the house and take a drive. Take a look at nature or local scenery. Find changing leaves in the fall, flowers blooming in the spring, and so on. Remember to bring some treats in case you get hungry.

29. **Have a video game night.** Grab some food and drinks and stay in for the night playing your favorite video games.

30. **Go bowling.** To make things a little more difficult, try bowling in different styles, such as using only your opposite hand, playing granny style, closing your eyes, etc.

31. **Make s'mores and read campfire stories.**

32. **Have a movie marathon.** Watch your favorite movies for a movie marathon. While you watch, munch on our Snickers Popcorn. The recipe is available at http://www.six sistersstuff.com/2012/01/super-bowl-snack -snickers-popcorn.html.

33. **Have a TV-show marathon.** Pick a TV show and get a whole season's worth of DVDs to watch together.

34. **Have a theme night.** Pick a theme for the night and center everything around it. For a Mexican night, you could eat Mexican food and go salsa dancing. Our Cheesy Enchilada Casserole (see page 16) would be the perfect addition to your evening.

35. **Try a new restaurant.** Pick somewhere neither of you have been and try it out.

36. **Take some lessons.** Try taking dance, pottery, or cooking lessons together.

37. **Restaurant hop.** Go to a different restaurant for each course of the meal: one stop each for an appetizer, main course, and dessert. Take turns picking where to go.

38. **Have a spa night.**

39. **Play 20 Questions.** Write a list of 20 questions to ask each other. Share your answers afterward.

40. **Make breakfast together and eat it in bed.**

41. **Exercise together.** Attend an exercise class at a local gym, take a walk or jog together, or do something active.

42. **Go for a test drive.** Head to your nearest car dealership and test drive your dream car.

43. **Take a hike.** Check out http://www.trails.com for a list of hiking trails in your area. Then choose one for your date-night hike.

44. **Break a record.** Read through the *Guinness Book of World Records* together and find something the two of you could potentially achieve as a couple and then do it together as a cheap date.

45. **Visit a bakery.** Go to a local bakery and pick out a treat for each other.

46. **Cook a meal together.** Find a recipe you've never tried and make it together. Be sure to include some dessert, like our Slow Cooker Hot Fudge Brownies (see page 57).

47. **Write a bucket list.** Make a list of things you both want to do before you die. And then go do one to cross it off the list.

48. **Go house hunting.** Tour some homes and plan out your dream home!

49. **Make a restaurant at home.** Find recipes from some of your favorite cookbooks or cooking websites, create a menu, and have a lovely meal at home.

50. **Go to the arcade.** Get some quarters and head to your nearest arcade. Play some games and buy prizes with the tickets you win.

Slow Cooker Hot Fudge Brownies

I recently moved from Missouri, where it was extremely hot and humid. The last thing I wanted to do was slave over a hot oven. I found this recipe, and my family loves it! The brownies are hot and gooey when they come out; I put a scoop of ice cream on top to make it the perfect summer treat!—Kristen

2 cups brownie mix	½ cup brown sugar
1 egg	2 tablespoons cocoa
1 tablespoon vegetable oil	¾ cup boiling water
¼ cup water	Chocolate frosting (optional)
⅓ cup milk chocolate chips	Vanilla ice cream (optional)

Combine brownie mix, egg, oil, water, and chocolate chips in a bowl. Spread batter in greased 3- to 4-quart slow cooker. In a small bowl, mix together brown sugar, cocoa, and boiling water, making sure to completely dissolve sugar and cocoa. Pour over batter. Cover and cook 2 hours on high heat. Turn off slow cooker and let sit for 30 minutes. Spoon into bowls and serve with ice cream and hot fudge. Refrigerate leftovers.

If you prefer frosting on your brownies, let them cool completely then spread on your favorite chocolate icing.

Makes 8 to 10 servings.

Slow Cooker Chicken Quesadillas

Craving something south of the border but don't have a lot of time? This simple slow cooker meal will have everyone wanting more at your fiesta!

⬦⬦

4 boneless, skinless chicken breasts	Tortillas
1 (14-ounce) can diced tomatoes, undrained	Shredded Monterey Jack cheese (or your favorite kind of cheese)
1 (4-ounce can) green chilies, drained	2 tablespoons melted butter (or olive oil)
1 (8-ounce) package cream cheese or Neufchatel	

Spray a slow cooker with nonstick cooking spray. Place chicken breasts in the slow cooker. Pour in diced tomatoes, green chilies, and cream cheese. Place the lid on the slow cooker and cook 6 to 8 hours on low or 3 to 4 hours on high. Once the chicken is cooked, remove from slow cooker and shred. Return chicken to slow cooker and mix well. If chicken seems too runny, drain off some of the liquid or use a slotted spoon to transfer mixture to tortillas. Keep chicken mixture warm until ready to make quesadillas.

To make quesadillas, heat a skillet over medium heat. Top one side of a tortilla with cheese and a scoop of the chicken mixture. Fold the tortilla over and press down. Lightly brush melted butter (or olive oil) on both sides. Cook two filled tortillas at a time, 3 to 4 minutes each, until they are golden brown, turning once.

Serve with your favorite salsa, guacamole, and sour cream.

Makes 4 to 6 servings.

Creamy Slow Cooker Ranch Pork Chops and Potatoes

These pork chops are juicy and tender, and the extra sauce makes perfect gravy. Because many people are concerned about preservatives and MSG in canned and packaged food, we've included recipes for homemade condensed soup and dry ranch seasoning as part of this recipe.

6 to 8 medium potatoes, chopped into large pieces

4 to 6 boneless pork chops

2 (10.75-ounce) cans condensed cream of chicken soup or homemade (see recipe at right)

2 packages dry ranch dressing mix or homemade (see recipe at right)

1 cup milk

Parsley flakes (optional)

Spray slow cooker with nonstick cooking spray and put potatoes on the bottom. Place pork chops on top of potatoes. Mix together the condensed soup, ranch dressing mix, and milk. Pour on top of the pork chops and cook on low 6 to 7 hours or on high 4 hours. Use the extra sauce in the slow cooker as a gravy for the potatoes and the pork chops. Sprinkle with dried parsley if you desire.

Makes 4 to 6 servings.

HOMEMADE CONDENSED CREAM OF CHICKEN SOUP

1½ cups chicken broth	⅛ teaspoon black pepper
1½ cups milk	¼ teaspoon salt (or less, taste to test)
½ teaspoon poultry seasoning	¼ teaspoon parsley flakes
¼ teaspoon onion powder	Dash of paprika
¼ teaspoon garlic powder	¾ cup flour (all-purpose or gluten-free flour)

In medium-sized saucepan, boil chicken broth, ½ cup milk, and the seasonings for a minute or two (longer if using fresh onions or garlic).

In a bowl, whisk together the remaining 1 cup milk and flour. Add to boiling mixture and continue whisking briskly until mixture boils and thickens. Yields 3 cups soup, which is equal to about 2 cans.

HOMEMADE RANCH DRESSING

2 tablespoons dried parsley flakes	1 teaspoon onion powder
1 teaspoon dried dill	½ teaspoon dried basil
1 teaspoon garlic powder	½ teaspoon pepper

Add each of the dried spices to a bowl and mix carefully. Store in a canning jar or resealable plastic bag. Recipe is equal to one packet of dry dressing mix.

Slow Cooker Chicken Cordon Bleu

You would never guess this dish came from a slow cooker! Layer your ingredients in your slow cooker, set the timer, and have an amazing meal by dinnertime!

- 1 (10.75-ounce) can cream of chicken soup
- 1 cup milk
- 6 boneless, skinless chicken breast halves
- 4 ounces sliced ham
- 4 ounces sliced Swiss cheese
- 1 (8-ounce) package herbed dry bread stuffing mix
- ¼ cup butter, melted

In a small bowl, combine cream of chicken soup and milk. Pour enough of the soup into a slow cooker to cover the bottom. Layer chicken breasts over the sauce. Cover with slices of ham and then Swiss cheese. Pour the remaining soup over the layers, stirring a little to distribute between layers. Sprinkle the stuffing on top and drizzle butter over stuffing. Cover and cook on low 4 to 6 hours, or 2 to 3 hours on high.

Makes 6 servings.

Slow Cooker Honey Sesame Chicken

This dish quickly became one of the most popular on our blog because it is simple to throw together, but tastes as though you spent all day preparing it. The honey in this recipe gives it the perfect amount of sweetness and flavor.

4 boneless, skinless chicken breasts
   Salt and pepper

1 cup honey

½ cup soy sauce

½ cup diced onion

¼ cup ketchup

2 tablespoons vegetable oil

2 cloves garlic, minced

¼ teaspoon red pepper flakes (optional)

4 teaspoons cornstarch

6 tablespoons water
   Sesame seeds

Season both sides of chicken breasts lightly with salt and pepper; place in slow cooker. In a small bowl, combine honey, soy sauce, onion, ketchup, oil, garlic, and pepper flakes. Pour over chicken. Cook on low 3 to 4 hours or on high 1½ to 2½ hours, or just until chicken is cooked through. Remove chicken from slow cooker, leaving sauce in ceramic insert. Dissolve cornstarch in water and pour into slow cooker. Stir to combine with sauce. Replace lid and cook sauce on high 10 more minutes or until slightly thickened. Cut chicken into bite-sized pieces, then return to pot and toss with sauce before serving. Sprinkle with sesame seeds and serve over rice or noodles.

Makes 4 to 6 servings.

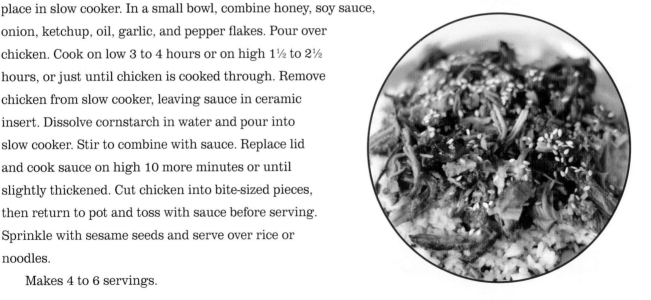

Slow Cooker Italian Chicken

This is a go-to meal in our family's meal rotation. Grown-ups and kids alike devour it and your family will never know you spent only a few minutes preparing dinner.

- 4 chicken breasts
- 1 packet dry zesty Italian dressing
- 1 (8-ounce) package cream cheese, softened

- 2 (10.75-ounce) cans cream of chicken soup
- 3 cups cooked rice or noodles

Place the chicken in a slow cooker and sprinkle Italian dressing over it. Combine cream cheese and cream of chicken soup in a small pot over low heat and warm until melted through; pour over chicken. Cook on low 4 to 6 hours. Once chicken is done, you can leave the chicken breasts whole or shred them. Serve chicken over pasta or rice.

Makes 6 servings.

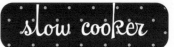

Slow Cooker Garlic and Brown Sugar Chicken

This recipe is so simple to make. Kids love it because it is slightly sweet, and adults can easily spice up their own servings with red pepper flakes. Serve this chicken over rice with a side of steamed vegetables to make a delectable meal even your picky eaters will love.

4 to 6	boneless, skinless chicken breasts	1	teaspoon fresh ground pepper
1	cup packed brown sugar	2	tablespoons cornstarch
⅔	cup vinegar	2	tablespoons water
¼	cup lemon-lime soda	4	cups cooked rice or noodles
2 to 3	tablespoons minced garlic		Red pepper flakes (optional)
2	tablespoons soy sauce		

Spray slow cooker with nonstick cooking spray. Place chicken breasts in slow cooker. Mix together brown sugar, vinegar, soda, garlic, soy sauce, and pepper in a small bowl. Pour over chicken. Cook on low 6 to 8 hours or high 4 hours. Take chicken pieces out of slow cooker and pour remaining sauce into saucepan. Place saucepan over high heat. Mix together cornstarch and water, pour into saucepan, and mix well. Let sauce come to a boil and cook 2 to 3 minutes, or until it starts to thicken and turns into a glaze. Remove from heat and let sit for a minute or two (it will continue to thicken as it cools down).

Serve chicken over rice or noodles and top with glaze. Sprinkle red pepper flakes on top if desired.

Makes 6 servings.

Homemade Fruit Snacks

Some of the first words out of my son's mouth were "fruit snacks!" He can't get enough of them. I decided to give homemade fruit snacks a whirl, and he loved them. This recipe uses gelatin, which means you can make a variety of different flavors. Using ice trays or gelatin molds, you can create many different fun shapes your little ones will love.—Elyse

1   (3-ounce) package gelatin, any flavor
2   (.25-ounce) envelopes unflavored gelatin
⅓   cup water

Sprinkle the gelatin over the water in a small saucepan. Heat over medium heat and stir until gelatin is completely dissolved. Pour into molds and allow to set at least 20 minutes.

The Best Fresh Spinach Dip

With only 5 ingredients, this refreshing dip is simple to create, and it pairs well with veggies for a great snack or appetizer.

1 (16-ounce) container sour cream

1 (8-ounce) package cream cheese, softened

1 (2-ounce) envelope dry onion soup mix

½ medium red onion, peeled and finely chopped

1 (10-ounce) bag fresh spinach, washed and drained well and shredded into smaller pieces

Mix all ingredients together, adding spinach last. Cover and chill in the refrigerator until ready to serve. Dip tastes best if you make it a couple of hours ahead and let the flavors combine. Tastes great with vegetables and crackers.

100

HEALTHY

SNACK IDEAS

1. Frozen grapes.

2. String cheese.

3. Bananas.

4. Frozen bananas. Peel a banana, insert a popsicle stick, pop it in the freezer overnight, and then enjoy a banana pop the next day.

5. Low-fat yogurt.

6. Sugar-free or fat-free pudding.

7. Apple slices dipped in peanut butter.

8. 100-calorie bag of popcorn.

9. Applesauce.

10. Raw veggies with hummus.

11. Almonds.

12. Apples.

13. Skinny s'mores. Place one roasted marshmallow and one small square dark chocolate between two graham crackers.

14. Smoked beef jerky.

15. Chocolate milk.

16. Hard-boiled eggs.

17. Sunflower seeds.

18. Cottage cheese.

19. Sliced cantaloupe.

20. Raisins.

21. Pita bread and hummus.

22. Rice cakes.

23. Sugar-free Jell-O.

24. Dried fruit.

25. Frozen Yoplait Whips Yogurt.

26. Air-popped popcorn.

27. Pistachios.

28. Clementines.

29. Handful of olives.

30. Pickles.

31. Orange slices.

32. **Kristen's Green Smoothie.** Check out the recipe at http://www.sixsistersstuff.com/2011/02/kristens-green-smoothies.html.

33. **Handful of blueberries with 2 tablespoons fat-free non-dairy whipped topping.**

34. **Ants on a Log (celery with peanut butter and raisins).**

35. **Mixed berry salad.** Toss one cup mixed berries (raspberries, strawberries, blueberries, and/or blackberries) with one tablespoon fresh-squeezed orange juice.

36. **Peanut butter and bananas on whole wheat bread.**

37. **Trail mix.** Make your own by tossing together dried fruit, sunflower seeds, nuts, low-sugar cereals, and a few pieces of candy for something sweet.

38. **Cherry tomatoes.**

39. **Graham crackers.** Dipped in skim milk.

40. **Small green salad with light dressing.**

41. **Mango smoothie.** Process frozen mango, mango Greek yogurt, and a small amount of orange juice together in a blender.

42. **Kebabs.** Thread low-fat meat, low-fat cheese, pineapple chunks, and cherry tomatoes onto a stick.

43. **Half of a cinnamon-raisin bagel topped with peanut butter and banana slices.**

44. **Grilled pineapple.**

45. **Baked apples.** Core an apple, fill the hole with 1 teaspoon brown sugar and 1 teaspoon cinnamon, bake at 350 degrees F. for about 30 minutes.

46. **Animal crackers.**

47. **Strawberries dipped in fat-free nondairy whipped topping.**

48. **Low-fat tortilla topped with egg salad, shredded carrots, and cucumber slices.**

49. **Yogurt parfaits.** Build your own with Greek yogurt or plain yogurt, fruit, and granola.

50. **Bowl of bran flakes with ½ cup skim milk and berries.**

51. **Guacamole with veggies.**

52. **Triscuit's Thin Crisps dipped in cottage cheese or hummus.**

53. **Cashews.**

54. **Pretzels.**

55. **Sun Chips.** Remember portion control! Read the serving amount on the side.

56. **Cheesy breaded tomatoes.** Two roasted plum tomatoes sliced and topped with 2 tablespoons breadcrumbs and a sprinkle of Parmesan cheese.

57. **Sugar snap peas.**

58. **Steamed veggies.** Steam non-starchy vegetables in a microwave-safe bag and sprinkle with 1 tablespoon Parmesan cheese or ¼ cup pasta sauce.

59. **Apricots.**

60. **Laughing Cow Light Cheese Wedges.**

61. **Any 100-calorie snack pack.**

62. **Granola bar.**

63. **Baked chips with salsa.**

64. **Soy chips.**

65. **Protein bar.**

66. **Sweet potato fries.** Slice one medium sweet potato, toss with 1 teaspoon olive oil, and baked at 400 degrees F. for 10 minutes.

67. **Tortilla wraps.** A slice of turkey, Swiss cheese, baby spinach leaves, and cranberry relish wrapped up in a whole-wheat tortilla.

68. **Pumpkin seeds.** 2 tablespoons pumpkin seeds, sprayed with oil and baked at for 400 degrees F. for 15 minutes or until brown. Sprinkle a tiny amount of salt on top.

69. **Bean salad.**

70. **Broccoli florets.**

71. **Peaches and cottage cheese.**

72. **Chopped red peppers dipped in fat-free ranch dressing.**

73. **V8 Vegetable Juice.**

74. **Tuna with Triscuit crackers.**

75. **Cooked and cubed chicken breast.**

76. **Homemade popsicles.** Puree watermelon, strawberries, mangos, bananas, and so on, and freeze in popsicle molds.

77. **Dates with almond butter or rolled in coconut.**

78. **Quesadillas.**

79. **Watermelon slices.**

80. **Cubed apples with cubed cheese on toothpicks.**

81. **Craisins.**

82. **Goldfish crackers.**

83. **Edamame.**

84. **Cheesy roasted asparagus.** 4 spears asparagus, spritzed with olive oil and topped with 2 tablespoons grated parmesan cheese, baked for 10 minutes at 400 degrees F.

85. **Turkey roll-ups.** 4 slices smoked turkey rolled up and dipped in 2 teaspoons honey mustard.

86. **Strawberry salad.** 1 cup raw spinach with ½ cup sliced strawberries and 1 tablespoon balsamic vinaigrette.

87. **Oatmeal.**

88. **Banana smoothie.** Mix ½ cup banana slices, ¼ cup nonfat vanilla yogurt, and a handful of ice. Blend until smooth.

89. **Lime sherbet.** (½ cup serving) with sliced kiwi.

90. **Apple chips (dehydrated apples).**

91. **Frozen mangoes.**

92. **Healthier Banana Bread.** Get the recipe at http://www.sixsistersstuff.com/2011/02/delicious-low-fat-banana-bread.html.

93. **Black beans.** Mix ¼ cup black beans with 1 tablespoon salsa and 1 tablespoon Greek yogurt for an added twist.

94. **Lettuce wrap.** Try 2 slices honey-baked ham with 2 teaspoons honey mustard rolled in a lettuce leaf.

95. **Pecans.** Try 5 pecans roasted with 2 teaspoons maple syrup and 1 teaspoon cinnamon.

96. **Chocolate-covered strawberries.** Dip 5 strawberries in 2 squares of melted dark chocolate.

97. **Honeyed yogurt.** One-half cup nonfat Greek yogurt with a dash of cinnamon and 1 teaspoon honey.

98. **Blackberries mixed with plain yogurt.**

99. **Tropical juice smoothie.** Blend ¼ cup each pineapple juice, orange juice, and apple juice with ice.

100. **Peanut Butter Yogurt Dip with fresh fruit.** Get the recipe at http://www.sixsistersstuff.com/2011/08/fruity-peanut-butter-yogurt-dip-recipe.html.

Tortilla Roll-Ups

These little roll-ups are the perfect appetizer and even make a great lunch!

◇◇◇

2 (8-ounce) packages of cream cheese, room temperature	Peas
1 (24-ounce) container sour cream	Diced carrots
2 to 3 tablespoons taco seasoning	Diced green peppers
1 (16-ounce) can refried beans	Chopped green onions
10 to 12 large tortillas	Niblets sweet corn
	Finely grated cheddar cheese

In a mixer, blend cream cheese and sour cream until smooth. Mix in taco seasoning. In the center of each tortilla, put a small stripe of refried beans. On the rest of the tortilla, spread the sauce, making sure to get to the edges. Use a decent amount to make sure all toppings will stick. Sprinkle with toppings and roll up. Be sure not to overstuff, or they won't roll up. Tuck in the ends and wrap in plastic wrap. Refrigerate overnight.

Slice before serving and serve with your favorite salsa.

Makes 40 roll-ups.

Twice-Baked Potato Casserole

Enjoy the delicious taste of a twice-baked potato in this simple casserole. With the bacon, potatoes, and cheese, you have one tasty side dish!

5 pounds russet potatoes	¼ cup minced chives
10 slices bacon	2½ cups grated cheddar cheese, divided
1 (8-ounce) package cream cheese	2 teaspoons kosher salt
½ cup unsalted butter, melted	½ teaspoon pepper
1 cup sour cream	

Preheat oven to 350 degrees F. Peel potatoes, and cut into 1-inch chunks. Place in a large saucepan and add enough cold water to cover by about 2 inches. Bring to a boil over medium-high heat, and then reduce to a simmer. Cook until tender and easily pierced with a paring knife, about 20 minutes. Transfer to a colander to drain; return to pan, cover, and set aside.

Meanwhile, heat a large skillet over medium heat. Add bacon and cook until crisp and browned, turning once. Transfer to paper towels to drain; let cool. Crumble into pieces.

Using a fork, mash the potatoes in pan until light and fluffy. Add cream cheese, butter, and sour cream, and stir until combined and smooth. Add chives, 2 cups cheddar cheese, half the bacon, salt, and pepper. Stir until well combined.

Transfer to a buttered, 3-quart baking dish. Top with remaining cheddar cheese. Bake until top is slightly golden and potatoes are heated through, about 30 minutes. Remove from oven; garnish with remaining bacon. Serve immediately.

Makes 6 to 8 servings.

Cheese Potatoes

We grew up eating these Cheese Potatoes and can't seem to get enough of them. They make the perfect side dish to any meal!

◇◇

4 to 6 potatoes

1 (10.75-ounce) can cream of chicken soup

¼ cup sour cream

¾ cup grated cheddar cheese

2 tablespoons melted butter

2 tablespoons chopped onion

Preheat oven to 350 degrees F. Peel and cut potatoes into chunks and boil in a large pot of water until tender; drain. Place cooked potatoes in a 9x9-inch glass pan. Combine soup, sour cream, cheese, melted butter, and chopped onion in a small bowl. Pour soup-cheese mixture over cooked potatoes. Bake 35 to 40 minutes.

Makes 4 to 6 servings.

Chinese Fried Rice

If you're looking for an Asian-inspired side dish, then you'll definitely want to try this! It is simple to make and full of flavor. If desired, throw in some diced ham or green onions as a variation.

3 tablespoons sesame oil	2 eggs, slightly beaten
1 cup frozen peas and carrots, thawed	4 cups cooked white rice
1 small onion, chopped	⅓ cup soy sauce
2 teaspoons minced garlic	

On medium-high heat, heat the oil in a large skillet or wok. Add the peas and carrots mix, onion, and garlic. Stir-fry until tender. Lower the heat to medium-low and push the mixture off to one side; pour beaten eggs on the other side of skillet and stir-fry until scrambled. Now add the rice and soy sauce and blend all together. Stir-fry until thoroughly heated.

Makes 6 to 8 servings.

Loaded Baked Potato Skins

If you love twice-baked potatoes, you have to try these potato skins. Topped with bacon, cheese, sour cream, and onions, these potatoes are fully loaded! My husband calls them "man-pleasing food" and tells me that the more bacon I use, the better.—Camille

4 large baking potatoes, baked

3 tablespoons olive oil

1 tablespoon grated Parmesan cheese

½ teaspoon salt

¼ teaspoon garlic powder

¼ teaspoon paprika

⅛ teaspoon pepper

8 bacon strips, cooked and crumbled

1½ cups shredded cheddar cheese

½ cup sour cream

4 green onions, sliced

Preheat oven to 475 degrees F. Grease a large baking sheet. Cut potatoes in half lengthwise; scoop out pulp, leaving a ¼-inch shell (save pulp for another use, or add butter, milk, and seasonings, mash it up, and serve as mashed potatoes). Place potato skins on prepared baking sheet. Combine oil, Parmesan cheese, salt, garlic powder, paprika, and pepper; brush over both sides of skins. Bake 7 minutes; turn over. Bake until crisp, about 7 minutes more. Sprinkle bacon and cheddar cheese inside skins. Bake 2 minutes longer or until the cheese is melted. Top with sour cream and onions. Serve immediately.

Makes 4 to 6 servings.

Low-fat Baked Onion Rings

You don't have to sacrifice flavor with this baked version of a fried favorite. Our Amazing Sauce adds a nice kick to this delicious side dish or snack.

4 Vidalia onions, sliced into rings	¼ teaspoon pepper
5 cups whole milk	½ teaspoon dried oregano
1½ cups Italian-style bread crumbs	¼ teaspoon cayenne pepper (optional)
½ cup crushed Ritz crackers	Amazing Sauce (see recipe below)
½ teaspoon salt	

Place sliced onions and milk in a bowl and let soak 1 to 2 hours in the refrigerator.

Preheat oven to 450 degrees F. Line baking sheet with parchment paper or foil. Combine bread crumbs, crushed cracker crumbs, salt, pepper, oregano, and cayenne pepper. Place half of crumb mixture in a bowl and reserve the other half to use later when the mixture in the first bowl begins to clump and doesn't stick as well to the onions. Dip each soaked onion ring into mixture and coat both sides with crumb mixture. Place rings onto baking sheet and bake 12 to 15 minutes until golden and the onion is soft. Serve immediately with Amazing Sauce.

Makes 3 to 4 servings.

AMAZING SAUCE

1½ cups brown sugar	4 tablespoons water
6 tablespoons Frank's hot buffalo sauce	1½ cups ranch dressing

Mix brown sugar, buffalo sauce, and water in a saucepan over medium heat until sugar is dissolved. Remove from heat and stir in ranch. Mix completely. Sauce may be stored in an airtight container for up to 5 days, refrigerated.

Fudgy Yogurt Fruit Dip

Just 3 simple ingredients and 5 minutes are all you need to make this incredible dip. If you love chocolate-dipped strawberries, this one is for you!

½ **cup hot fudge ice cream topping**

½ **cup vanilla yogurt**

1½ **teaspoons frozen orange juice concentrate, thawed**

Fresh strawberries, bananas, pineapple, and other fruit for dipping

In a bowl, combine fudge topping, yogurt, and orange juice concentrate. Cover and refrigerate for at least 30 minutes (or, if you are in a hurry, place it in the freezer for about 10 minutes). Serve with fruit.

14

DAYS OF

VALENTINES

This is more of a project than a craft, but it's certain to make Valentine's Day special for a special someone. Give the gifts in any order. The printables associated with each gift are available at http://www.sixsistersstuff .com/2012/01/14-days-of-valentines-with -free.html

INSTRUCTIONS

Day 1: You are the apple of my eye!

For a gift, use dried apples, apple juice, candy apple rings, or actual apples.

Day 2: Honey, comb your hair, because we've got a date tonight!

You could also save this one until Valentine's Day and go on a date that evening. For a gift, you could use Honeycomb cereal or an actual hair comb.

Day 3: You are one hot tamale!

For a gift, use Hot Tamales, Red Hots, or any other cinnamon candy.

Day 4: I'm nuts about you!

For a gift, use any type of nuts, a Nutrageous candy bar, or Nutter Butter cookies.

Day 5: I wouldn't chews anyone but you!

For a gift, use gum, Starburst fruit chews, Charleston Chews, or chewy granola bars.

Day 6: I think you are *soda*mazing!

For a gift, use a can of soda, soda candies, or soda crackers.

Day 7: We were mint to be together!

For a gift, use breath mints, York Peppermint Patties, butter mints, or a mint-flavored dessert.

Day 8: We make a great combo!

For a gift, use combo baked snacks, a combination pizza, or PB&J combo jars.

Day 9: Thanks for sticking by my side!

For a gift, use a tube of ChapStick, Chic-O-Sticks, orange or raspberry sticks, or super glue.

Day 10: I'm bananas for you!

For a gift, use a Banana Colada Fuze, real bananas, or banana-flavored candy

Day 11: You have o*fish*ally stolen my heart!

For a gift, use Swedish Fish or Goldfish crackers.

Day 12: I would be so mixed up without you!

For a gift, use any flavor of Chex Mix, trail mix, or other snack mix.

Day 13: Life would be unbearable without you!

For a gift, use a bag of gummy bears, a honey bear, Klondike Bars with the bear on the front (just be sure to keep them in the freezer), or a teddy bear.

Day 14: You make my heart bubble over!

For a gift, use a bottle of sparkling cider, sparkling water, or any type of carbonated beverage.

Grilled Chicken Bow Tie Pasta Salad

Need to get your kids to eat their veggies? This dish is the solution to your problem. My kids don't even notice the vegetables mixed in with the other yummy ingredients. It is simple to make with leftover grilled chicken or shredded rotisserie chicken.—Camille

1 (12-ounce) package bow tie pasta

2 cups fresh broccoli florets

2 to 3 cups chopped, grilled chicken

1 cup halved cherry tomatoes, or 1 large tomato cut into chunks

1 green pepper, cut into small pieces

1 cup Italian salad dressing (we love Wishbone Robusto Italian)

4 ounces Colby Jack cheese, cut into tiny bite-sized pieces

1 (2.25-ounce) can sliced black olives

¼ cup grated Parmesan cheese

Cook pasta according to package directions, adding broccoli to the cooking water for the last 2 minutes. Drain water. Toss chicken, tomatoes, pepper, dressing, cheese, and olives together in a large bowl. Add pasta and broccoli, toss lightly. Sprinkle with Parmesan cheese and serve.

Makes 6 to 8 servings.

Oriental Chicken Salad

This super-easy recipe is simple to assemble, and the dressing is delicious. Save your money and make this restaurant-quality meal for your family at home.

- 6 tablespoons honey
- 3 tablespoons rice vinegar
- ½ cup mayonnaise
- 2 teaspoons Dijon mustard
- ¼ teaspoon sesame oil
- 2 pieces of crispy chicken strips (frozen or from the deli) or leftover grilled chicken

- Bagged salad with assorted lettuces, cabbage, and vegetables
- Bagged broccoli slaw
- 1 tablespoon sliced almonds, toasted
- ¼ cup fried wonton strips (optional)
- ¼ cup mandarin orange slices, drained well

Prepare dressing first by blending together honey, rice vinegar, mayonnaise, Dijon mustard, and sesame oil with a wire whisk or mixer. Refrigerate while you work on the salad.

Bake the chicken strips according to the package directions if frozen, or reheat grilled or deli chicken. Cut up the chicken into bite-sized pieces.

Mix together a large handful of the lettuce salad and the broccoli slaw. Top with cut-up chicken, almonds, wontons and mandarin slices. Drizzle the dressing on top. Serve immediately.

Makes 4 servings.

Strawberry Spinach Salad and Homemade Poppy Seed Dressing

This refreshing salad is colorful, fresh, and simple to put together. The homemade poppy seed dressing is packed with flavor and accents all the other ingredients. When strawberries are not in season, this salad is delicious with mandarin oranges. You can also throw in a grilled chicken breast and turn this salad into a main dish.

2 tablespoons sesame seeds

1 tablespoon poppy seeds

⅓ cup sugar

½ cup olive oil

¼ cup distilled white vinegar

¼ teaspoon paprika

¼ teaspoon Worcestershire sauce

Dash of fresh ground pepper

1 tablespoon minced red onion

10 ounces fresh spinach, rinsed, dried and torn into bite-size pieces

1 quart strawberries, cleaned, hulled and sliced

¼ cup chopped walnuts

Bacon bits

Red onion slices for the top (optional)

Feta cheese or bleu cheese to sprinkle on top (optional)

In a blender, process sesame seeds, poppy seeds, sugar, olive oil, vinegar, paprika, Worcestershire sauce, pepper, and minced onion. Blend until the onion is pureed. Pour the dressing into a bowl, cover, and chill for at least an hour.

In a large bowl, combine spinach, strawberries, walnuts, bacon bits, red onion slices, and cheese. Toss lightly. Pour dressing over salad right before you are ready to eat so that the spinach does not wilt.

Makes 4 to 6 servings.

Southwest Salad

I'm trying to eat healthy, but I have to admit that I am terrible at making salads. So I found a recipe I liked and changed it a little bit. I serve the salad with homemade wheat bread for a super quick, super easy, and super yummy meal!—Kristen

1   (10-ounce) bag of romaine salad (spinach would also work)

1   avocado, sliced

1   tomato, diced

1   (15-ounce) can of black beans, drained

1   cup corn

1   cup sliced olives

1   pound (about 2 chicken breasts) seasoned chicken (I use the precooked southwestern seasoned chicken found by the deli meat)

Fat-free garlic vinaigrette olive oil dressing (I like Paula Dean's)

Toss salad ingredients with fat-free dressing and serve with warm homemade wheat bread.

Orange Fluff Jell-O Salad

Every Sunday, our mom would make some sort of Jell-O as a side dish to our delicious dinner. This recipe was one of our favorites growing up. It makes a lot so it is great as a salad, side dish, or dessert for parties or big dinners.

1 (6-ounce) package cook-and-serve vanilla pudding

1 (6-ounce) package orange gelatin

2 cups water

1 (16-ounce) container nondairy whipped topping

1 (10-ounce) bag mini marshmallows

1 can pineapple tidbits (any size), drained

1 can mandarin oranges (any size), drained

2 bananas, sliced (optional)

Combine pudding mix, Jell-O, and water in a saucepan over medium heat and bring to a boil. Remove from heat and pour into a large mixing bowl. Refrigerate until mixture has thickened, about an hour. Beat until creamy. Fold in whipped topping, marshmallows, and all fruit except bananas. Chill about an hour before serving. If using bananas, stir in right before serving so they don't turn brown.

Makes 8 to 10 servings.

Grandma's Five-Cup Creamy Fruit Salad

Our cute Grandma A. is an amazing cook! Many of our best recipes are from her kitchen. This fruit salad was a staple at most family get-togethers, and the best part about it is that you don't have to have any experience in the kitchen to whip it up. It is just a matter of pouring five ingredients in a bowl and mixing them together.

1 (11-ounce) can mandarin oranges, drained

1 (8-ounce) can crushed pineapple, drained

1 to 2 cups miniature marshmallows

1 cup flaked coconut

1 cup sour cream

Combine oranges, pineapple, marshmallows, coconut, and sour cream. Make sure fruit is well drained so you don't have a watery salad. Stir until it's all mixed together. Refrigerate 4 to 8 hours before serving.

Makes 6 servings.

Five-Minute Fluffy Yogurt Fruit Salad

This recipe really takes only five minutes to throw together—no kidding! It's the perfect side dish to any meal and is always a hit at potlucks. If you use canned or frozen fruit, drain really well so salad is not runny.

- 2 (6-ounce) containers yogurt, any fruit flavor
- 1 (8-ounce) container nondairy whipped topping
- 1 (10-ounce) bag mini marshmallows

  Fresh, frozen, or canned fruit that complements your yogurt flavor

Dump yogurt into a bowl. Fold in the container of whipped topping and mix well. Add marshmallows and fruit. Chill for 30 minutes and serve.

Makes 6 servings.

Snickers Apple Pudding Salad

This is the perfect snack or side dish for a hot summer day! Kids love it, and it is also a big hit at barbecues and potlucks. The crunchy apples and chewy candy bar pieces are the perfect complement to the pudding base.

1 cup milk

1 (6-ounce) package vanilla instant pudding

1 (16-ounce) container nondairy whipped topping

6 regular-sized Snickers candy bars, cut in bite-sized pieces

3 medium Granny Smith apples or other tart apple, cut up into small chunks

In a large bowl, combine milk and pudding, and then mix in the whipped topping. Add the Snickers and the apples. Chill for 1 hour before serving.

Makes 6 to 8 servings.

101

FUN, EASY, AND CHEAP INDOOR ACTIVITIES FOR KIDS

1. **Have an indoor picnic.**

2. **Build a fort out of blankets.** Use chairs, couches, yarn—anything to hold up the blankets.

3. **Make sock puppets.**

4. **Finger paint with pudding.**

5. **Use rolling pins and cookie cutters to make Play-Doh shapes.**

6. **Have a dance party to your favorite songs.**

7. **Have a tea party.**

8. **Read nursery rhymes.**

9. **Make your own indoor hopscotch with masking tape on carpet or wood.**

10. **If you have little girls, give them pedicures.**

11. **Play school and let your child be the teacher.**

12. **Make a letter book.** Let the kids take a picture of something that starts with each letter of the alphabet.

13. **Look through old photo albums.**

14. **Make a movie of yourselves and then watch it.**

15. **Paint with watercolors.**

16. **Play with Barbies.**

17. **Play with Matchbox cars.** Visit http://www.sixsisters stuff.com/2011/11/cozy -matchbox-car-caddy-mat -tutorial.html to learn how to make our fun Matchbox car caddy mat.

18. **Play board games.**

19. **Color with crayons.** Take off the wrappers and experiment with different ways you can color with them.

20. **Make paper bag puppets.**

21. **Watch a movie and eat popcorn.**

22. **Go on a treasure hunt.**

23. **Bake cookies.**

24. **Play dress-up.**

25. **Make paper hats.**

26. **Make a healthy snack.**

27. **Make a relay race or obstacle course in your house—be creative!**

28. **Play hide-and-seek.**

29. **Have an indoor snowball fight.** Use rolled-up socks for snowballs.

30. **Build a fort out of cardboard boxes and duct tape.**

31. **Make plans and invitations for a party.**

32. **Play tic-tac-toe.**

33. **Make your own puzzle out of poster board or cardstock.** Color it, cut it out, and put it back together.

34. **Make your own matching game.**

35. **Swim in the kitchen.** Put down a tarp, fill up a kiddie pool with warm water, and let them play for hours!

36. **Make Valentine's Day décor.**

37. **Make a car track all around your house with masking tape.**

38. **Play "Monster in the Middle."** Pillows are *safe*; the carpet is the *lava*. Jump from pillow to pillow; if the monster touches you, you are in the middle.

39. **Make apple stamps.** Cut an apple in half horizontally and use it as a stamp using washable paint.

40. **Make lacing cards with favorite cereal boxes.**

41. **Learn a new song.**

42. **Create a giant dot-to-dot with poster board.**

43. **Make homemade valentines.**

44. **Make a necklace with yarn, beads, or Froot Loops.**

45. **Have a talent show.**

46. **Cut out paper snowflakes.**

47. **Make a paper countdown chain.** Pick an upcoming birthday or holiday and cut strips of paper and staple them together in a chain to be removed one at a time leading up to the event.

48. **Put out some hard noodles, Elmer's glue, and paper and let the kids be creative.**

49. **Have marble races.** Take 2 swimming pool water noodles and prop them on the stairs. Race marbles down the middle of them. The hole is a perfect size for a marble.

50. **Sculpt clay, let it dry, and then paint your creations.**

51. **Play with paper dolls.**

52. **Write letters to grandma and grandpa.**

53. **Play with magnets.** Cut up colorful pipe cleaners into 1-inch pieces, put them in a glass jar, hold a magnet to the outside of the jar, and see what happens!

54. **Make a countdown calendar for an upcoming holiday.**

55. **Build a city out of Legos or other blocks.** Or have a contest to see who can build the tallest, freestanding tower.

56. **Make princess or king crowns.** Use our Felt Crown tutorial at http://www.six sistersstuff.com/2011/03 /cute-felt-birthday-crown.html.

57. **Take silly pictures.** E-mail them to Dad or Mom at work.

58. **Make big cars out of cardboard boxes.** Have the kids sit inside the boxes, cut holes in the cardboard for their legs, and let them use their feet as wheels to move around.

59. **Play red-light, green-light.** Play this with the cars you make in #58. It is so fun!

60. **Toilet paper a room in your house.**

61. **Make an Ice Sun Catcher.** Take a pie tin and fill it with water, leaves, pine cones, and yarn so it can hang. Then put it outside (if it's winter) or in the freezer and let it freeze. When it is frozen, take it out and hang it on a tree.

62. **Build a pillow pile.** Collect all the pillows in your house and jump into them.

63. **Dress up in Mom's or Dad's clothes.**

64. **Plan a date for your child and you (or spouse) that makes them feel special.**

65. **Paint with shaving cream.** Put shaving cream and drops of food coloring in a cookie tray and then mix it all around with a paintbrush.

66. **Make a storybook out of paper.** Have kids make up the story and draw the pictures.

67. **Watch old family videos.**

68. **Have a fire drill.** Organize and practice your family's plan in case of a fire. Practice stopping, dropping, and rolling.

69. **Make paper airplanes.**

70. **Make a toilet paper trail.** Give each kid a roll and have them make a trail all around the house.

71. **Read favorite books.**

72. **Start a journal.** If your children are too young to write, have them tell you what to write.

73. **Make a time capsule of their favorite things.** Open it next January.

74. **Make flash cards (letters, sounds, addition, etc.).**

75. **Make homemade paper dolls.** Visit http://www.sixsisters stuff.com/2011/06/free-paper -doll-printables-perfect.html for printable paper dolls.

76. **Make cupcakes.** Let the kids do the decorating themselves.

77. **Plan a family vacation.**

78. **Teach the kids to sew.**

79. **Do an exercise video.**

80. **Rearrange the furniture in the kids' bedrooms.**

81. **Make a hot cocoa bar.** Use chocolate-covered spoons, marshmallows, whipped cream, and Andes mints. Get creative!

82. **Make a bird feeder with a toilet paper roll.** Spread peanut butter on the empty toilet paper

roll. Coat the peanut butter in bird seed, and use yarn to hang it outside. Watch the birds come.

83. **Make little pizzas.** Use English muffins, tomato sauce, cheese, and any toppings you want. Cook at 350 degrees F. until cheese melts.

84. **Put on a play.**

85. **Make a superhero costume out of household items.** Check out our No-Sew T-Shirt Cape tutorial at http://www.sixsistersstuff.com/2011/04/no-sew-t-shirt-super-hero-capes.html.

86. **Color the snow.** Scoop up a few buckets or tubs of snow. Bring it in the house and fill squirt bottles with warm water and food coloring. See what designs you can make in the snow-filled buckets.

87. **Let the kids use your makeup to give you a makeover!**

88. **Let the kids pick and print out coloring pages online.**

89. **Make a piñata and fill it with yummy (or healthy) treats.**

90. **Have a campout in the front room . . .** tent and all.

91. **Play doctor.**

92. **Play Mummy Wrap.** Have your kids work together to wrap you, or another child, up in toilet paper.

93. **Make and frost sugar cookies.** Try our delicious Sugar Cookies recipe available at http://www.sixsistersstuff.com/2011/03/delicious-soft-sugar-cookies.html.

94. **Make a ball toss.** Set out a few different-sized buckets and have kids throw balls into them. For older kids, fill the buckets with water almost to the top. It is a lot harder than it seems.

95. **Put lipstick on your kids and have them make a kiss card for Dad or grandparents.**

96. **Read a book and then act out the story.**

97. **Play a game of indoor bowling.** Stuff socks into toilet paper rolls and line them up. Roll a ball into them and you have your own bowling alley!

98. **Fill up the sink!** Add some dish soap, cups, spoons, bowls, and anything else that isn't breakable. Just make sure there are a couple of towels under their chairs, and let them go at it.

99. **Play grocery store with items from your pantry.** Let the kids check out with plastic bags.

100. **Give the kids a creative bath!** Put in toys you usually don't let go in the tub (that are still waterproof) and let the kids play.

101. **Chore race.** Have the kids each draw a chore from a hat and then compete to see who can finish their chore first.

Easy Blackberry and Cream Cheese Danish

To say we love this recipe would be an understatement! It takes just a couple of minutes to put together, but tastes like it came straight from a pastry shop. It makes a great breakfast or dessert! You can actually fill this pastry with any kind of fruit, or just use the cream cheese filling without the fruit—that would be yummy too!

1 (8-ounce) package cream cheese, softened	1 can refrigerated crescent rolls
½ cup granulated sugar	1 cup fresh blackberries or 1 cup blackberry pie filling
3 tablespoons all-purpose flour	½ cup powdered sugar
1⅛ teaspoons vanilla, divided	2 tablespoons heavy cream

Preheat oven to 375 degrees F. In a small bowl, combine cream cheese, sugar, flour, and 1 teaspoon vanilla. Set aside. Pop open crescent roll dough and unroll, leaving crescents in rectangles. On an ungreased baking sheet, lay the crescent roll rectangles together, lining them up widthwise. Dough should be almost the entire length of a half-sheet pan. Press edges together to even out edges and seal any holes. Cut ½-inch diagonal strips up each side of the dough. Carefully spread cream cheese filling down the center of the dough, about 2- to 3-inches wide. Top with fresh blackberries. Fold ½-inch dough pieces up over filling, alternating sides to get a braided pattern. You may have excess dough once you reach the end, so fold it in as best as you can. Bake 15 to 20 minutes or until filling is set and crescent dough is golden in color. Cool before removing from baking sheet.

Once Danish has cooled, move to serving platter. In a small bowl, mix together powdered sugar, remaining vanilla, and cream to create icing. You may need to add more cream to get the desired consistency. Drizzle icing over Danish. Cut into pieces and serve.

Makes 4 to 6 servings.

Mini Maple Pancake Muffins

This fun twist on pancakes is sure to please everyone in the family.

1 cup all-purpose flour	⅔ cup buttermilk
1 teaspoon baking powder	1 egg
½ teaspoon baking soda	3 tablespoons pure maple syrup
¼ teaspoon salt	2 tablespoons melted butter
3 tablespoons sugar	½ cup milk chocolate chips

Preheat oven to 350 degrees F. Generously grease a 24-cup mini muffin pan with nonstick spray. Whisk together flour, baking powder, baking soda, salt, and sugar in a medium bowl. In another bowl, stir buttermilk, egg, maple syrup, and melted butter until just combined. Add wet ingredients to dry ingredients and stir with a spoon until combined. Stir in chocolate chips. Reserve a few chips to sprinkle on the tops. Bake 8 to 9 minutes.

Let cool slightly and remove from the pan. You may need to use a toothpick around the edges to separate the pancake muffins from the pan.

Makes 24 mini pancake muffins.

FELT

BOWS

The best part of these bows is that no sewing is required—all you need is a glue gun. They also can be made in about 10 minutes, so pull out some felt scraps, plug in your glue gun, and get started.

SUPPLIES

- free, printable template
- felt
- scissors
- straight pins
- hot glue

http://www.sixsistersstuff
.com/2012/07/felt-bow-hairbow
-tutorial-and-free.html

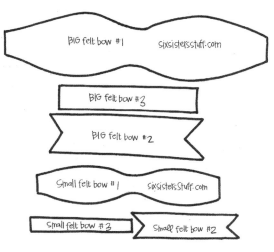

Felt Bow Template
SixSistersStuff.com

BIG felt bow #1   sixsistersstuff.com

BIG felt bow #3

BIG felt bow #2

Small felt bow #1   sixsistersstuff.com

Small felt bow #3   Small felt bow #2

INSTRUCTIONS

1. Cut out pattern.

2. Pin on pattern. Using straight pins, secure pattern pieces to felt.

3. Cut out felt. Follow the pattern to cut out felt pieces.

4. Glue large bow piece together. Put a tiny dot of glue on one end of the large bow piece (on the pattern, this piece is labeled Big felt bow #1). Bring the ends together so they form a bow shape. Hold in place until glue dries.

5. Attach piece #3. Put a small dot of glue in the middle of the piece of felt that matches the pattern piece labeled Big felt bow #3. Attach to the bow as pictured.

Big felt bow #2 to the center of the bow. Flip bow over, place a small dot of glue on back, and wrap piece #2 around to the glue. Hold until glue dries. Use another dot of glue to glue down the other end of piece #2.

7. Trim excess. Trim off any excess as needed.

8. Repeat. Repeat for small bows and as many additional bows as you'd like.

6. Attach piece #2. Use a small dot of glue to attach the felt piece made from the pattern piece labeled

Blueberry Cake Mix Muffins

This recipe makes soft, moist muffins using a cake mix. These are quick and easy to make and can be varied with different ingredients, such as blackberries, raspberries, or even chocolate chips.

1 (15.25-ounce) box yellow or white cake mix

1 teaspoon baking powder

2 tablespoons all-purpose flour

⅔ cup milk

⅓ cup vegetable oil

3 large eggs

1 to 2 cups fresh blueberries

Preheat oven to 375 degrees F. Mix dry cake mix, baking powder, flour, milk, oil, and eggs together thoroughly. Fold in the blueberries very gently. Leave a couple out so that you can sprinkle them on top. Only stir a couple of times so that your batter doesn't turn blue or purple.

Pour into lined muffin cups (fill about ⅔ full) and bake 15 to 20 minutes. For chocolate muffins, use a chocolate cake mix and add one cup chocolate chips instead of berries.

Makes 16 to 18 muffins.

Cake Mix Cinnamon Rolls

Cinnamon rolls can be a little intimidating, but these Cake Mix Cinnamon Rolls are foolproof! Using a box of cake mix in this recipe takes these cinnamon rolls over the top with just the right amount of sweetness!

2 tablespoons active dry yeast (two packets)

2½ cups warm water

1 (15.25-ounce) box white or yellow cake mix

1 teaspoon salt

5 cups all-purpose flour

1 teaspoon vanilla

1½ cups brown sugar

½ tablespoon cinnamon

¼ cup butter, softened

1 (16-ounce) can cream cheese frosting

In a small bowl, mix yeast and warm water until dissolved; set aside. Combine cake mix, salt, and flour in a large bowl. Add warm water-yeast mixture and vanilla and stir well. This may require kneading with your hands a bit to completely combine ingredients. Cover bowl tightly and let rise for one hour. Punch down and let rise again for another 30 to 60 minutes.

On a floured surface, roll dough into a rectangle shape, approximately ¼-inch thick. Once dough is rolled out, brush with softened butter. Sprinkle with brown sugar. Sprinkle with cinnamon—use as little or as much as you like. Starting at end opposite from you, roll the dough toward you until all dough is rolled into one long roll. Slice dough into 24 equal-sized pieces.

Preheat oven to 350 degrees F. Place rolls in two greased 9×13-inch pans. Cover and let rise until doubled in size. (We usually set rolls on the stovetop while the oven preheats.) Bake 15 to 25 minutes or until golden brown. This will depend on your stove and how brown you like your cinnamon rolls. Remove from oven and let cool slightly. If you prefer your frosting to melt into your rolls, frost after rolls have cooled 10 to 15 minutes. If you prefer your frosting to stay on top of your rolls, wait to frost until rolls have cooled.

Makes 24 rolls.

Easy 7-Up Biscuits

These biscuits are so easy, your kids can help make them. The 7-Up makes the biscuits so soft and fluffy that no one will know they aren't made from scratch!

½ cup sour cream

2 cups Bisquick baking mix, plus extra for dusting countertops

½ cup 7-Up

¼ cup butter, melted

Preheat oven to 450 degrees F. Cut sour cream into biscuit mix with a fork. Add 7-Up and stir just until combined. It makes a very soft dough. Sprinkle extra biscuit mix on counter or table and pat dough out. Don't knead the dough, just pat it out. Pour melted butter in a 9-inch square pan. Cut dough into 9 circles. Place cut biscuits in prepared pan and bake 12 minutes or until golden brown. Keep an eye on them during the last minutes of cooking.

Makes 12 biscuits.

Three-Ingredient Easy Parmesan Rolls

We love anything quick, easy, and delicious. If you're looking for an easy side dish, these are right up your alley! These have been a family favorite for years!

¼ cup butter

½ cup grated Parmesan cheese (fresh or canned)

8 rise-and-bake frozen rolls (such as Rhodes)

Place butter in a microwave-safe dish and heat until completely melted. Place grated Parmesan in a separate dish. Dip each frozen roll completely in butter, and then roll in grated Parmesan until covered.

Place rolls on a greased pan and allow to rise until doubled (follow directions on package). Bake according to package directions until rolls are golden on top.

Makes 8 rolls.

BUILD YOUR 72-HOUR KIT IN 52 WEEKS

Building a 72-hour kit can seem daunting, but this week-by-week plan can help ease your fears. If you want to put your kits together in less than a year, do two or three of the assignments each week and have the kits ready in a fraction of the time!

Prepare a separate bag for each member of your family, even the small children. For most weeks' assignments, add the suggested item to *each* family member's kit, as appropriate. Some of the items listed are not appropriate for children (matches, knives, etc.) and should, therefore, be placed in only the parents' kits. Other items, such as duct tape, paper towels, baby wipes, etc., might not be necessary for each family member and may weigh down bags for smaller kids. Just add what you think is best to each bag, but remember that you may get separated from each other in an emergency so it's best that each person have his or her own pack with necessities. Anything on this list can be substituted to suit the needs of your family.

Week 1: Obtain suitable 72-hour-kit containers (backpacks, duffel bags, plastic totes with lids, etc.). Have one for each member of your family.

Week 2: Check and replace the batteries in your smoke detector. Practice escape routes with your family and have an emergency plan.

Week 3: Place a flashlight next to your bed and one in an alternate location; check batteries. Place a flashlight in each of your children's rooms and let them know where it is.

Week 4: Add 3 gallons of water to each 72-hour kit (the Red Cross recommends 1 gallon per person per day). Water takes up a lot of room in a pack, so you might want to put only a few water bottles in each pack (maybe about a gallon's worth) and keep the rest in containers that can be carried in your arms. Decide what will be best for your family. Sometimes clean water is the most rare commodity in emergencies—not only will it be used for drinking, but also for cleaning. The Red Cross also recommends having a 2-week supply of water in your home, just in case clean water is not available.

Week 5: Add $10 cash to each 72-hour kit (the smaller the bills, the better). If you have a large family and this seems difficult, add $5 cash each time this assignment comes up. Having cash on hand is extremely important in emergencies, especially when computer systems might be down and debit and credit card transactions and ATM withdrawals can't be made.

Week 6: Add a manual can opener.

Week 7: Add 2 cans tuna fish or other canned meat.

Week 8: Add 1 roll paper towels.

Week 9: Add 1 emergency blanket.

Week 10: Add $10 cash to each 72-hour kit.

Week 11: Add 4 rolls toilet paper.

Week 12: Add 1 bar of soap.

Week 13: Add 1 or 2 stress-relief factors to each kit (books, magazines, coloring books, playing cards, games, crossword puzzles, Sudoku, etc).

Week 14: Add pocket or utility knife (Swiss army knife).

Week 15: Add $10 cash to each kit.

Week 16: Add 1 container baby wipes.

Week 17: Add 1 change of clothing, including underwear and socks.

Week 18: Add a few nonperishable, easy-to-prepare food items, such as granola bars, oatmeal bars, trail mix, beef jerky, canned ravioli, etc. Date for rotation. Get enough to last for at least 3 days.

Week 19: Add 1 can of fruit and 1 can of vegetables. Date for rotation. Make sure they have the pull-tab on top for easy opening.

Week 20: Add $10 cash to each kit.

Week 21: Add 1 box waterproof matches and 1 lighter.

Week 22: Add hard candy, such as Jolly Ranchers, Lifesavers, etc.

Week 23: Add 1 small jar peanut butter (or other protein).

Week 24: Add zipper-lock bags (variety of sizes).

Week 25: Add $10 cash to each kit.

Week 26: Check the batteries in your smoke detector. Practice escape routes with your family and have an emergency plan.

Week 27: Add 1 box crackers and 1 large can non-carbonated fruit juice.

Week 28: Add plastic utensils, paper plates, and a couple of paper cups.

Week 29: Add 1 roll duct tape.

Week 30: Add $10 cash to each kit.

Week 31: Add 1 box graham crackers.

Week 32: Add a flashlight and extra batteries.

Week 33: Add disinfectants (Betadine, bleach, sterile wipes, hand sanitizer).

Week 34: Add 1 pair work gloves.

Week 35: Add $10 cash to each kit.

Week 36: Add basic first-aid kit.

Week 37: Add 1 pound dried fruit. Date for rotation.

Week 38: Add ½ pound dried milk and one box cereal.

Week 39: Add battery-powered or hand-crank radio (add extra batteries if it is battery powered)

Week 40: Add $10 cash to each kit.

Week 41: Add items related to individual medical needs, such as hearing aids, glasses, contact lenses, syringes, canes, etc.

Week 42: Add feminine hygiene products, and other hygiene products. If you have a baby, add diapers, bottles, formula, and baby food. If you have a pet, add pet supplies (collar, leash, ID, food, bowl, etc).

Week 43: Add toothbrush and 1 tube toothpaste.

Week 44: Add a multi-purpose tool.

Week 45: Add $10 cash to each kit.

Week 46: Verify that each family member's immunizations (especially tetanus shots) are up to date.

Week 47: Purchase additional cell phone chargers for cell phones in your home.

Week 48: Add a pair of scissors.

Week 49: Add an emergency candle.

Week 50: Add $10 cash to each kit.

Week 51: Make copies of house keys and car keys to keep in a kit.

Week 52: Add photocopies of personal documents, such as wills, insurance policies, birth certificates, medication lists and other medical info, proof of address, deed/lease to home, passports, marriage license, etc. Keeping each document in plastic sleeves inside a three-ring binder will help keep the documents organized. You might consider sending 1 copy of each document to a trusted family member/friend in a separate location. Also add a map of the area and an emergency contact card (with local phone numbers and phone numbers of friends/family outside of the area) to each kit. Keep pictures of family members in each kit in case you get separated and need to ask if anyone has seen them.

Additional supplies to keep at home or in your kit based on the types of disasters common to your area:

Whistle

Small hand axe

N95 or surgical masks

Rain gear

Towels

Tools/supplies for securing your home

Extra clothing, hat, and sturdy shoes

Plastic sheeting

Household liquid bleach

Blankets or sleeping bags

Two-way radios

Hand warmers

Portable fuel source

Light sticks (makes a great night light, especially for children)

Pair of flip-flops (in case you have to leave in such a hurry that you can't grab shoes)

30-Minute Dinner Rolls

1 cup plus 2 tablespoons warm water

⅓ cup vegetable oil

2 tablespoons active dry yeast (two packets)

¼ cup sugar

½ teaspoon salt

1 egg

3½ cups all-purpose flour, divided

Preheat oven to 400 degrees F. In the bowl of a standing mixer, combine warm water, oil, yeast, and sugar; let rest for 5 to 10 minutes or until mixture is frothy and bubbly. Attach mixer's dough hook and mix in salt, egg, and 2 cups of flour until combined. Add remaining flour a little at a time (dough will be sticky). Spray your hands with cooking spray and shape the dough into 12 balls. After rolls are shaped, place on lightly greased cookie sheet and let rest for 10 minutes. Bake 10 minutes or until tops are lightly golden.

Makes 12 rolls.

Easy Parmesan Knots

This recipe is so easy and tastes so good that your family will think you whipped 'em up from scratch! You'd never guess they take only 15 minutes.

1	can refrigerated buttermilk biscuits	1	teaspoon garlic powder
¼	cup canola oil	1	teaspoon dried oregano
3	tablespoons grated Parmesan cheese	1	teaspoon dried parsley flakes

Preheat oven to 400 degrees F. Grease a large baking sheet. Cut each biscuit into thirds. Roll each piece into a 3-inch rope and tie into a knot; tuck ends under. Place 2 inches apart on prepared baking sheet. Bake 8 to 10 minutes or until golden brown.

In a large bowl, combine the remaining ingredients; add the warm knots and gently toss to coat.

Makes 30 knots.

Cheesy Garlic Sticks

We love the big pieces of garlic Texas Toast you buy in the freezer section of the grocery store. But we don't love the nutritional facts on the side of the box, so we decided to make something that tastes just as great but without the extra fat and calories.

1 **(13.8-ounce) can refrigerated pizza dough**

Olive oil for brushing dough

2 **cups shredded mozzarella cheese**

1 **tablespoon minced garlic**

Italian seasoning

Preheat oven to 425 degrees F. Roll out pizza dough on a baking pan. Brush dough lightly all over with olive oil. Sprinkle shredded mozzarella all over dough. Use your fingers and sprinkle minced garlic all over the dough. Sprinkle Italian seasoning on the top, as desired. Bake 12 to 18 minutes. Cut into 1-inch strips and serve.

Makes 12 to 24 breadsticks, depending on how small you slice them.

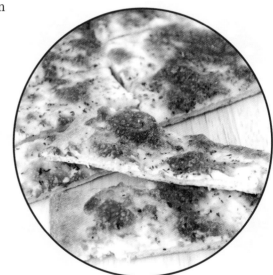

Easy Homemade Rolls

Many roll recipes involve periods of letting the dough rise, kneading it, and following complicated instructions, but these rolls don't need any of that! Our Easy Homemade Rolls require very little preparation but taste like you spent all day in the kitchen.

◇◇◇

1 tablespoon active dry yeast (one packet)	½ cup butter, melted
½ cup sugar	½ teaspoon salt
3 eggs, beaten	4 cups all-purpose flour
1 cup lukewarm water	

Mix yeast, sugar, eggs, water, butter, and salt together in a large bowl. Add flour. Mix well with a spoon, cover bowl with plastic wrap, and allow dough to rise 4 to 6 hours or overnight in the refrigerator. Do not knead the dough.

Preheat oven to 375 degrees F. Turn out dough onto a lightly floured surface and divide in half. Roll each half of dough into a circle. Brush with additional melted butter and cut into 16 pieces, like a pizza. Roll up each piece from the large end to the point. Pinch tip of dough into roll so it doesn't come loose. Place rolls on a cookie sheet and let rise 30 to 60 minutes. Bake 8 to 10 minutes.

Makes 3 dozen rolls.

Mom's Strawberry Freezer Jam

Our mom whipped out a million batches of this jam every summer, and we would eat it year-round. If you have ever wanted to try homemade jam, this recipe is simple and fail-proof! You can use the same recipe for peach, apricot, and raspberry jam. This jam tastes amazing on hot bread and makes a great gift for friends and neighbors.

3 pounds strawberries, washed and hulled

¼ cup lemon juice

1 (2-ounce) box pectin

1 cup light corn syrup

4 cups sugar

Place strawberries in a large, microwave-safe bowl. Mash strawberries with a potato masher; if you like chunky jam, leave more chunks as you mash. Add lemon juice. Slowly add the package of pectin, about ⅓ at a time, mixing between each addition. Stir until pectin is mixed in completely. Let sit 30 minutes at room temperature.

Stir in corn syrup and then sugar, 1 cup at a time. Stir well between each cup of sugar. Place bowl in microwave and heat on high 4 to 5 minutes (uncovered), until it starts to bubble around the edges.

Stir mixture and pour into clean jars or plastic freezer containers. Leave jam sitting out at room temperature 1 to 2 hours to cool down before putting in the freezer.

Makes about 2 quarts.

STAINED

MASON JARS

Stained Mason jars make beautiful flower vases or decorative holders for treasures and trinkets. Do not, however, store anything you plan on eating in these jars because the Mod Podge makes them unsafe. You can use water in them for plants.

SUPPLIES

- Mason jar
- 2 tablespoons water
- 4 tablespoons Mod Podge
- food coloring
- paper plate
- spoon
- waxed paper
- baking sheet

INSTRUCTIONS

1. **Preheat oven to 200 degrees F.**

2. **Prepare Mod Podge.** Mix water and Mod Podge together on a paper plate, and then add as many drops food coloring as needed to reach desired shade and color (jar above used 5 drops blue food coloring).

3. **Color the jar.** Pour all of the water and Mod Podge mixture into the Mason jar. Move the jar around, making sure to coat the whole inside of the jar. Now, pour all of the water and Mod Podge mixture out of the jar, making sure it coats the mouth of the jar as it drips out. Wipe the outside edge of the jar to remove any drips. Be sure there is only a thin

layer on the inside of the jar; otherwise, the color will not come out even.

4. **Set the coating.** Place the jar upside down on a cookie sheet lined with waxed paper and place it in the oven for 3 minutes. Remove the baking sheet from the oven and turn the jar upright. Wipe rim carefully with a paper towel to remove excess water and Mod Podge mixture. Return the jar (upright) on the cookie sheet to the oven. Bake until the color is clear and beautiful, about 30 to 40 minutes. Add a ribbon or flowers to your jar for some extra flair!

Chocolate Chip Banana Oatmeal Cookies

These are so chewy and delicious you'll want to let your bananas turn brown just so you can make them!

◇◇

- 2 cups all-purpose flour
- 1 teaspoon salt
- ½ teaspoon baking soda
- ¾ cup unsalted butter, softened
- ½ cup granulated sugar
- ½ cup packed brown sugar
- 1 egg

- 1½ teaspoons vanilla
- ½ cup mashed ripe banana (about 1 large banana)
- 1 cup old-fashioned rolled or quick-cooking oats
- 2 cups chocolate chips

Preheat oven to 375 degrees F. Whisk together flour, salt, and baking soda in a small bowl and set aside. Place butter and sugars in a mixing bowl and beat on medium speed until pale and fluffy. Reduce speed to low. Add egg and vanilla and mix until combined. Mix in banana. Add flour mixture and mix until just combined. Stir in oats and chocolate chips. Using a 1½-inch ice cream or cookie scoop, drop dough onto baking sheets, spacing about 2 inches apart. Bake cookies until golden brown and just set, about 12 to 13 minutes.

Makes 4 to 5 dozen cookies.

Orange Creamsicle Cookies

These cookies taste just like biting into a delightful orange Creamsicle!

2½ cups all-purpose flour

¾ teaspoon baking soda

½ teaspoon salt

1 cup butter, softened

½ cup granulated sugar

½ cup firmly packed brown sugar

1 large egg

1 teaspoon vanilla

2 tablespoons orange zest

2 cups white chocolate chips

Preheat oven to 375 degrees F. In a small bowl, combine flour, baking soda, and salt; set aside.

In a large bowl, cream butter and sugars together until light and creamy. Beat in egg and vanilla until smooth. Gradually add flour mixture until combined. Stir in orange zest and white chocolate chips. Drop rounded teaspoonfuls onto ungreased cookie sheets. Do not flatten cookies; it will make them dry. Bake 8 to 10 minutes or until golden brown around edges. Do not overcook! Cookies will be plump. Cool for several minutes on cookie sheets before transferring to rack to cool completely. Store in airtight container.

Makes 3 to 4 dozen cookies.

40

ROAD TRIP

IDEAS FOR KIDS

1. **Print off a checklist of all fifty states and let the kids cross off states when they see the corresponding license plates.** Visit http://www.thedatingdivas.com/tara/the-road-trip-date/ to find a cute, printable list of license plates.

2. **Buy some window markers and let the kids go to town on the back windows.** When finished, they can wipe the windows clean with a baby wipe or disposable glass-cleaning wipes.

3. **Pack a small pad of paper and colored pencils inside a DVD case.** The hard case also makes the perfect writing surface!

4. **Give your kids glow sticks, glow necklaces, or glow bracelets when traveling at night.**

5. **Play the Lines and Dots game.** Directions and printables are available at http://www.momsminivan.com/printables.html.

6. **Purchase inexpensive clipboards at the dollar store and let the kids decorate them with markers and stickers.** They can then use the clipboards as hard writing and coloring surfaces.

7. **Make Pencil Pouch I-Spy bags before you leave.** Find our easy tutorial at http://www.sixsistersstuff.com/2011/05/no-sew-i-spy-bag-and-quiet-book.html.

8. **Go to your local library and check out some audio books on CD to listen to on the drive.**

9. **Wrap a couple of small toys or trinkets from the dollar store and let the kids choose one every couple of hours.** These are great to use as incentives to keep your kids good in the car!

10. **Purchase one of those candy-filled toys your kids always beg for in the checkout lines.** Yes, they are kind of expensive, but for long trips, a candy-filled camera or an electronic sucker spinner can entertain little ones for nearly an hour. Definitely worth the dollar or two to buy them!

11. **Print out some fun Mad Libs for the drive.** Visit www.classroomjr.com/printable-mad-libs-for-kids/ to find several Mad Lib options to print.

12. **Have the kids make stained-glass window pictures.** Fold a piece of paper at an angle and then unfold it, making a nice crease. Fold the paper again and unfold. Repeat this until you have a page with several sections. Color in each shape with a different color crayon to make it look like a stained glass window.

13. **Buy a clear, plastic box with a lid and turn it into a craft kit.** Let the kids decorate the kit with stickers and glitter pens, and then fill the box with age-appropriate supplies they can use on the drive.

14. **Buy an inexpensive cookie sheet and make our Magnet Board on the Go.** A tutorial can be found at http://www.sixsisersstuff.com/2011/03/magnet-boards-on-go.html.

15. **Use the same cookie sheet as a hard surface for coloring (the edges keep the crayons from rolling away), playing Matchbox cars, building simple Lego sets, or keeping other small items from falling on the floor.**

16. **Purchase some cheap magnetic letters and numbers from the dollar store and let the kids spell words on the cookie sheet.**

17. **Bring some pipe cleaners and let the kids bend them, make shapes, mold stick people, make jewelry, and so on.** Kids love things they can be creative with.

18. **Pack some little snack bags with Fruit Loops cereal and let the kids string it on pipe cleaners (it's much easier than yarn).** Doubles as a great snack!

19. **Play the Alphabet Game.** Choose a topic, such as boys' names, girls' names, song titles, food, and so on. Then go around the car and have each person name something in that category that starts with the letter A. Move to the letter B, and then the letter C, and so on. Give each person 15 to 20 seconds to come up with an answer before moving on to the next person. Hand out small candies or snacks, such as M&M's or a cracker each time a person makes it through a round without getting stuck.

20. **Make up a travel scavenger game.** Kids can look for certain objects, listen for particular sounds, or even recognize smells. To print off a premade scavenger hunt for older kids, visit http://www.momsminivan.com/print-scavenger.html. A scavenger hunt for preschoolers can be printed from http://www.momsminivan.com/print-scavenger-preschool.html.

21. **Bring a stack of toy catalogs for the kids to leaf through on the drive.** We love the Fat Brain Toys

Holiday catalog. You can subscribe to it for free at http://www.fatbraintoys.com/catalog/index.cfm.

22. **Designate a long road trip as one of those rare occasions when your family's regular food rules don't apply.** Every once in a while cookies and candy are acceptable, and letting the kids indulge on road trips can be just the trick to keeping kids happy.

23. **Prepare paper dolls.** Print off the cute paper dolls available at http://www.sixsistersstuff.com/2011/06/free-paper-doll-printables-perfect.html before you leave.

If you want, mount them on magnetic sheets and use them on your cookie sheet.

24. **Purchase a new coloring book and box of crayons for each child.** Never underestimate the power of a new coloring book!

25. **Bring a roll of aluminum foil and let the kids make animals, people, shapes, etc.** Just don't let them bunch it into balls and start a throwing fight.

26. **Give each child a new notebook and let them draw pictures, put in stickers, take notes, tape in tickets or other memorabilia from your trip.**

Add pictures you took from your camera at the end of your trip for a fun keepsake.

27. **Play Road Trip Bingo.** Have little prizes for the winners. Search the web for printable bingo cards. Several are available at http://www.momsminivan.com/printables.html.

28. **Make your own dry erase board by covering a cookie sheet with white Contact paper.** Bring along some dry erase markers and a rag to use as an eraser.

29. **Make a kid-friendly playlist for the car.**

30. **Play the game 20 Questions as a family.**

31. **Make your own binder of activity pages.** Fill a 3-ring binder with clear plastic sleeves. In the sleeves, put blank papers, and some simple games (hangman, tic-tac-toe, word searches, find the hidden pictures, and connect-the-dots). Use a 3-ring pencil bag to hold the dry erase markers and a rag to use as an eraser. The kids can doodle and play for hours, then wipe the sleeves clean.

32. **Give each child an inexpensive disposable camera (or maybe a kid-safe or old digital camera, if you have one) and let them document the vacation and road trip.**

33. **Purchase some sticker books or activity books from the dollar store.**

34. **Make some paper bag puppets and then put on a puppet show during the drive.** We love the ideas at http://www.dltk-kids.com/type/paper_bag.htm.

35. **Play "Would You Rather . . ."** Each person in the car takes turns asking the others funny questions, such as "Would you rather sleep on the ground or on a bunk bed that is 10 feet tall?" or "Would you rather be a kangaroo or a turtle?" A quick search on the web can help you find questions if you don't want to come up with them yourself.

36. **Bring along some fun travel-friendly games, such as Hedbanz, Uno, or Go Fish!**

37. **Make a behavior clip for each kid.** Attach the clips to the sun visor. If a child misbehaves, whines, acts out, etc., remove the clip until the next rest stop. Let the kids know that whoever still has a clip on the sun visor at the next rest stop gets a treat. We like the tutorial at http://the-wilson-world.blogspot.com/2012/05/roadtrip-ready-roadtrip-behavior-clips.html.

38. **Pass out reward tickets.** Buy a roll of carnival tickets at a party store and use them as travel tickets. If a child behaves well, helps a younger sibling, or follows certain directions, give him or her a travel ticket. Let the kids cash in their travel tickets for specific prizes, such as 1 hour on Mom's iPad, a candy bar, a small toy, etc.

39. **Make Homemade Gak before you leave.** It takes only 2 minutes to throw together, doesn't leave a mess behind, and provides lots of entertainment! A tutorial is available at http://crafts.kaboose.com/homemade-kids-gooey-gak.html

40. **Have a family spelling bee or trivia contest.** Have each family member write down a couple of words or questions. When someone answers correctly, award them with small prizes such as stickers, activity or coloring books, trading cards, small treats, or extra minutes of hotel pool time or stay-up-late time.

Root Beer Float Cookies

These cookies are super soft and moist, and the frosting on top is what makes the cookie. If you love root beer, you will love these cookies!

1 cup butter, softened	4 cups all-purpose flour
2 cups packed brown sugar	1 teaspoon baking soda
2 eggs	1 teaspoon salt
1 cup buttermilk	Root Beer Frosting (see recipe below)
1 teaspoon root beer extract or concentrate	

Preheat oven to 375 degrees F. In a mixing bowl, cream together butter and brown sugar. Add eggs one at a time, beating well after each addition. Beat in buttermilk and root beer extract.

Combine dry ingredients in a separate bowl and gradually add to creamed mixture. Drop by tablespoonfuls onto ungreased baking sheets. Bake 10 to 12 minutes or until lightly browned. Remove to wire racks to cool. Frost and serve.

Makes 3 to 4 dozen cookies, depending on size.

ROOT BEER FROSTING

4 cups powdered sugar	3 tablespoons milk
¾ cup butter, softened	1 teaspoon root beer extract or concentrate

In a mixing bowl, combine all ingredients. Beat until smooth.

Mini Sugar Cookie Fruit Pizzas

Our mom has been making this treat for us since we were little. It's her famous sugar cookie recipe with a sweet, cream cheese layer and a fresh-fruit topping. This counts as healthy food, right? Get the kids involved by letting them top the individual pizzas however they want.

1 cup butter or margarine, softened

1¼ cups granulated sugar

2 eggs

2 teaspoons vanilla, divided

4 cups all-purpose flour

1 teaspoon baking powder

1 teaspoon baking soda

½ teaspoon salt

¼ cup milk

1 (8-ounce) package cream cheese, softened

1 cup powdered sugar

1 (8-ounce) container nondairy whipped topping

Sliced strawberries

Sliced kiwi

Sliced bananas

Grapes

Blueberries

Mandarin orange segments

Raspberries

Pineapple chunks

Preheat oven to 350 degrees F. In a large bowl, cream together butter, sugar, eggs, and 1 teaspoon vanilla. Mix in flour, baking powder, baking soda, salt, and milk. Chill dough for an hour. Once chilled, roll out dough on a floured surface until it's a little more than ¼-inch thick. Use round cookie cutters to cut out mini pizzas. Place on ungreased cookie sheets and bake 13 minutes. Let the sugar cookie crusts cool completely.

In a small bowl, beat cream cheese, powdered sugar, and 1 teaspoon vanilla until smooth. Fold in whipped topping. Spread cream cheese layer over cooled sugar cookies. Add fruit as desired.

Makes 2 to 3 dozen mini pizzas, depending on size.

DO-IT-YOURSELF ICE CREAM CONE PIÑATA

Making your own piñata can add the perfect finishing touch to a fun party. This piñata is great for birthdays, summer celebrations, or any occasion you need to party. Remember to start the piñata a week ahead of time so the papier-mâché layers have time to dry.

SUPPLIES

- 1 balloon blown-up to a 10-inch diameter
- newspaper cut or torn into 1½ x 9-inch strips
- 1 cup flour
- 1 cup water
- rope
- poster board
- super glue
- 1 roll tan or brown crepe paper
- 2 rolls pink crepe paper, cut into squares
- Elmer's glue

INSTRUCTIONS

1. **Make a paste.** Mix flour and water together in a large bowl to make a paste.

2. **Cover balloon.** Place your balloon on a small glass bowl or something that will keep it standing upright. Dip a strip of newspaper into the paste mixture and cover it completely in paste. Run the newspaper strip through two of your fingers to remove excess paste (and yes, your hands will be a mess when you are done!). Completely cover all of the exposed balloon with newspaper strips and let it dry. (Stick it in the sunshine or over a heating vent for quicker drying time!) Let it dry several hours or overnight.

3. **Finish covering.** Once the balloon is dry, flip it over and cover the exposed balloon with more strips of paste-covered newspaper. (You'll need to make a new batch of paste for each layer added.) Let dry completely. Depending on how strong and thick you want your piñata, add more layers of newspaper, repeating the above steps. Two layers will do, but big parties with lots of kids call for 4 or 5 layers so every kid gets a couple of turns to whack the piñata.

4. **Attach a rope.** Decide what end will be the top of the piñata. Cut two small holes in the top so that you can run a rope through to hang your piñata. Also, cut another small hole in the top so that you can pour candy and small toys inside. When you cut your holes, it will pop the balloon on the inside of the papier-mâché shape, so try and fish out the deflated balloon.

5. **Make a cone.** Use a large piece of poster board and roll it into a cone shape. Make sure the opening of the cone fits the bottom of the ice cream shape well, and then glue or staple the poster board together to maintain its cone shape. Use super glue to attach

the cone to the dried ice cream top. Hold in place while it dries.

6. **Cover the cone.** Unroll a section of tan or brown crepe paper (don't cut it off) and place a line of Elmer's glue along the top. Starting at the tip of the cone, wrap the crepe paper around and around the cone shape, adding more glue as you go. Wrap it all the way to the top of the cone.

7. **Cover the ice cream.** Using an unsharpened pencil, place the pencil in the middle of a small square of crepe paper. Wrap the crepe paper around the pencil. There is really no rhyme or reason to this, and you can experiment with how tight or loose you like the pieces to look on the piñata. Dip the flat end of the square of crepe paper (still wrapped around the pencil) in a little bit of Elmer's school

glue. Place the small square of crepe paper on the piñata . . . and repeat . . . and repeat . . . and repeat a couple hundred more times. It is easier to finish the top of the piñata when it is hanging so that the rest of the crepe paper is not smashed.

8. **Fill with candy.** Fill the finished product with candy, hang securely, and hit away!

EASY RUFFLE-KNOTTED HEADBAND

Even moms need something ruffly for their hair! This easy-to-make headband is perfect when you want to add a little flair to your hair.

SUPPLIES

- **headband**
- **matching sheer fabric (just a small scrap will do)**
- **scissors**

INSTRUCTIONS

1. **Make strips.** Cut 20 1x4-inch fabric strips.

2. **Attach strips to headband.** Tie each strip in a knot onto the headband. Continue to tie the strips to the headband—that will create a "ruffle" effect to the fabric. In the pictured headband, the knots are tied down the side so the ruffle would be on the side, rather than straight across the middle of the headband, but you can position the ruffle anywhere you want.

3. **Trim ruffles.** Trim down the ruffle to even it out.

Sugar Cookie Bars

Making, cutting out, and frosting sugar cookies can take most of the day, but this recipe gives you a sugar cookie fix without all the hard work. This recipe is basically one huge sugar cookie baked on one cookie sheet. The prep time and bake time are incredibly short—and you only have to frost one large cookie!

1 cup unsalted butter, room temperature	5 cups all-purpose flour
2 cups granulated sugar	1 teaspoon salt
4 large eggs	½ teaspoon baking soda
2 teaspoons vanilla	Mom's Frosting (see recipe below)

Preheat oven to 375 degrees F. Grease a half jelly roll pan or another 13x18x1-inch rimmed pan.

In a large bowl, cream butter and sugar with an electric mixer until fluffy. Add eggs one at a time, mixing after each addition. Stir in vanilla.

In a separate bowl, whisk together flour, salt, and baking soda. Add to wet mixture and mix just until combined. Spread on baking sheet. The dough will be just like cookie dough—heavy and sticky—so it helps to spray your hands with a little nonstick spray and then mold the dough into the pan.

Bake 10 to 15 minutes, until light golden brown or until a toothpick comes out clean. Cool completely before frosting with Mom's Frosting. Cut into bars and serve.

Makes 16 to 24 bars, depending on size.

MOM'S FROSTING

½ cup butter, softened	4 to 5 cups powdered sugar
¼ cup milk	Food coloring (optional)
2 teaspoons vanilla	

Combine all ingredients until well blended. Add more or less powdered sugar, according to desired consistency.

No-Bake Peanut Butter Bars

These take about 5 minutes to throw together and can then chill in the refrigerator until after dinner for a delicious dessert.

1 cup butter, melted

2 cups graham cracker crumbs

2 cups powdered sugar

1 cup plus 4 tablespoons peanut butter, divided

1½ cups milk chocolate chips

In a medium bowl, mix together melted butter, graham cracker crumbs, powdered sugar, and 1 cup peanut butter until well blended. Press evenly into the bottom of an ungreased 9x9-inch square pan. (If you prefer a thinner bar, use a 9x13-inch pan.) In the microwave, melt the chocolate chips with the remaining peanut butter at 50 percent power, stirring every 30 seconds until melted and smooth. Spread over the peanut butter layer. Refrigerate for at least one hour before cutting into squares.

Makes 9 thick bars or 15 thin bars.

Andes Mint Cookies

These cookies are so decadent and warm and gooey—be warned, you will need a glass of milk to go with them. They're also great to share . . . or not. ☺

1 **(15.25-ounce) box devil's food cake mix**

½ **cup oil**

2 **eggs**

1 **(8-ounce) bag Andes mints**

Preheat oven to 350 degrees. In a large bowl, mix cake mix, oil, and eggs together. Drop spoonfuls of dough onto baking sheet. Bake for 6 to 9 minutes.

Take baking sheet out of oven and, while the cookies are still hot, place an Andes Mint on top of each one. In about 5 minutes, the mint will be melted. Smooth out each melted mint like frosting.

Makes 3 dozen cookies.

Lunch Lady Peanut Butter Bars

I don't know about you, but at my elementary school they served amazing desserts. Sometimes I find myself craving the lunch ladies' chocolate cake or homemade cinnamon rolls. Elyse gave me this recipe from Mom's old recipe box, and it is seriously spot-on to what the lunch ladies served!—Camille

1 cup granulated sugar	2 cups oats (not quick-cooking)
1 cup firmly packed brown sugar	2 cups all-purpose flour
1 cup butter, softened	1 teaspoon baking soda
1 teaspoon vanilla	1 teaspoon salt
2 eggs	Mom's Chocolate Frosting (see recipe on page 160)
2½ cups peanut butter, divided	

Preheat oven to 350 degrees F. Grease a 13x8-inch jelly roll pan.

In a large bowl, cream together sugars and butter. Add vanilla, eggs, and 1 cup peanut butter, and mix well. Stir in oats, flour, baking soda, and salt. Spread dough on prepared pan and bake 15 minutes, until golden brown. While hot, spread remaining 1½ cups peanut butter on top. Cool so that the peanut butter solidifies again. (I usually chill them in the fridge so they set up faster and I can eat them sooner!) Spread Mom's Chocolate Frosting on top, and cut into bars.

Makes 24 bars.

DO-IT-YOURSELF STACKED FRAMES

What better way to add a little color to a room than with picture frames? For the wood, consider buying 1 long board at a hardware store and having it cut into 3 pieces of the right size. Also, feel free to use larger or smaller pieces of wood and frames.

SUPPLIES

- 3 16x24-inch pieces of wood
- 3 8x10-inch picture frames
- paint (such as spray paint and/or acrylic paint)
- painter's tape
- wood gel stain
- foam paint brushes
- medium-fine grit sandpaper
- industrial-strength Velcro (found at a hardware store)
- 3 8x10-inch pieces foam board
- sawtooth hangers

INSTRUCTIONS

1. **Prep picture frames.** Remove all hardware from picture frames, including the little metal clamps that hold on the back of the frame.

2. **Paint boards and frames.** Paint frames and boards as desired. The boards shown here were sprayed with two coats of paint: Krylon Flat White for the white board and Krylon Blue Ocean Breeze for the blue boards. The blue frame was sprayed with 2 coats of paint, and the orange frames were painted with Folk Art Acrylic Paint in Tangerine, applied with a foam paint brush. Let frames and boards dry thoroughly before moving to step 3.

3. **Sand frames and boards.** After paint has dried, use sandpaper to sand down the edges of the frames and boards. If desired, run the sandpaper all over the front of the wood boards to give them a bit of a distressed look. Use a clean cloth to wipe off the dust after sanding so you have a clean surface to work with.

4. **Add stripes.** Use painter's tape to mark off horizontal stripes on the boards. Place the stripes any distance apart; or use a different design, such as polka dots or vertical stripes. The stripes on the pictured boards were made with 2 coats of Folk Art Acrylic Paint in Tangerine. Let paint dry, remove tape, and use sandpaper to achieve a distressed look.

5. **Apply gel stain.** Using a foam paint brush, apply a swipe of gel stain to a frame. Spread the gel stain on a few inches at a time. Otherwise, it will dry too quickly.

Using a clean rag, quickly wipe away the gel stain after just a few seconds. It will leave the stain in the cracks and divots, giving the frame a distressed look. Do this to all three frames.

Apply gel stain to the boards as well. They will absorb the stain more quickly, so it might look a little scary for a minute; don't worry!

6. **Sand again.** Sand down edges and fronts of each piece of wood. This gives the wood an antiqued look and gets rid of the brush marks from where the stain was applied. After you have sanded everything to your liking, wipe the boards down with a clean cloth to remove all dust.

7. **Apply industrial-strength Velcro.** Put a strip of Velcro on the top and bottom of each frame, making sure the fuzzy size of the Velcro is facing forward. For extra security, you can also attach Velcro to the sides of each frame.

Place a frame on a board in the position you would like it to appear when finished. Use a pencil to lightly mark where to place Velcro on the board. Glue Velcro, with the scratchy side facing out, in the marked locations. Repeat with each board and frame.

8. **Apply a sawtooth hanger to the back of each board.**

9. **Insert photographs.** Place down glass from each original frame, then place down your picture. Top with the foam backing.

10. **Attach frames.** Line frames up with Velcro on each board and attach.

Better-Than-Anything Brownies

We come from a long line of chocolate lovers, so we know a good brownie when we taste one. All kinds of rich, gooey flavors combine to make this brownie, which just might be better than anything!

1 (15.25-ounce) package German chocolate cake mix

¾ cup butter, melted

1 (5¾-ounce) can evaporated milk, divided

1 (14-ounce) bag caramels

1 (8-ounce) bag Heath toffee bits, divided

1 (12-ounce) bag milk chocolate chips, divided

Grease a 9x13-inch baking pan. Preheat oven to 350 degrees F. In a large bowl, mix together cake mix, melted butter, and ⅓ cup evaporated milk. Press half of this mixture into prepared pan. Bake 6 minutes. Meanwhile, melt together caramels and remaining evaporated milk in a small saucepan over medium-low heat, stirring often. Remove brownies from oven after 6 minutes and sprinkle on half the bag of Heath toffee bits. Pour melted caramel over toffee bits. Sprinkle on half the bag of chocolate chips. Spread the remaining batter on top (this is easiest if you take pieces of the batter, flatten each individual piece in your hands and place on top). Sprinkle remaining toffee bits and chocolate chips on top. Bake 20 minutes. Cool on a wire rack and then refrigerate for 3 hours before serving.

Makes 24 brownies.

Mom's Chocolate Marshmallow Brownies

When we were growing up, our mom would make these brownies all the time, but it was always for someone's birthday or for a sick neighbor or for a friend . . . never for us! When mom did make a pan just for our family, it was always a special treat. And we could eat the whole pan in a matter of hours. They are perfect to share with neighbors or take to a potluck party. Or, eat the whole pan if you feel like it. We won't judge you.

1 cup margarine or butter, softened	1 teaspoon salt
2 cups sugar	2 teaspoons vanilla
⅓ cup cocoa	1 (10-ounce) package miniature marshmallows
4 eggs	Mom's Chocolate Frosting (see recipe below)
1½ cups all-purpose flour	

Preheat oven to 350 degrees F. Grease a 10x15 rimmed baking sheet.

Cream together margarine, sugar, and cocoa in a large bowl. Add eggs, one at a time, mixing well after each addition. Add flour, salt, and vanilla and mix well. Spread on prepared baking sheet. Bake 22 to 25 minutes. Brownies are done when a toothpick inserted in the middle comes out clean. Remove from oven and cover entire top with miniature marshmallows. Return to oven for 3 minutes, until marshmallows are soft and puffy. Cool and frost with Mom's Chocolate Frosting.

Makes 2 to 3 dozen brownies.

MOM'S CHOCOLATE FROSTING

½ cup butter or margarine, softened	3 tablespoons cocoa
¼ cup milk	2 to 3 cups powdered sugar
1 to 2 teaspoons vanilla, depending on your taste	

Beat all ingredients with an electric mixer until smooth. Add more powdered sugar or milk until you reach desired consistency.

German Chocolate Cake Bars

These little bars are the perfect alternative to baking a full cake when you crave that German-chocolate-cake taste but don't want to eat more than a few bites. Bake a pan of these bars, eat 1 or 2, and then share the rest with friends and neighbors. They will love them!

½ cup unsalted butter, melted

1 (15.25-ounce) box devil's food cake mix (not the kind with pudding added)

2 large eggs, divided

1 (14-ounce) can sweetened condensed milk

1 teaspoon vanilla

1 cup chopped pecans

1 cup shredded coconut

½ cup milk chocolate chips

Preheat oven to 350 degrees F. Grease a 9x13-inch baking pan. In a medium bowl, mix together butter, cake mix, and 1 egg. Press into the bottom of the prepared pan without pushing the crust up the sides. Bake for 7 minutes and remove from the oven. The crust will not look done; that's okay.

While the crust is baking, mix together sweetened condensed milk, 1 egg, vanilla, pecans, and coconut. Pour over the warm crust and sprinkle with the chocolate chips. Bake 24 to 30 minutes, or until the top is a light golden brown. Remove from the oven and cool completely before cutting.

Makes 2 dozen bars.

M&M's Blondies

These blondies are rich and brown sugary . . . and with the cute M&M's on top, they are hard to resist.

10 tablespoons unsalted butter

1 cup packed dark brown sugar

¼ cup granulated sugar

1 large egg

2 teaspoons vanilla

¼ teaspoon kosher salt

1¼ cups all-purpose flour

1¼ cups sweetened flaked coconut

1¼ cups M&M's (mini or regular), plus more for topping

Preheat oven to 350 degrees F. Coat an 8x8-inch pan with nonstick cooking spray and then line the bottom with parchment paper.

Heat butter in a small saucepan over medium heat until it browns and begins to smell nutty (watch it closely so it doesn't burn). Let the butter cool for a few minutes, until just barely warm.

In a large mixing bowl, combine the browned butter and sugars. With a wooden spoon, stir in egg, vanilla, and salt. Stir in flour, coconut, and M&M's until batter is blended.

Pour the batter into the prepared pan and smooth the top with a rubber spatula. Sprinkle a few additional M&M's on top. For slightly gooey, underbaked blondies, bake for 25 minutes. For fully baked blondies, bake the entire 30 minutes. Let the blondies cool before turning them out onto a cutting board and slicing into squares (chilling them will make that process even easier).

Makes 16 bars.

S'mores Bars

My sweet husband always wants to go camping. As a child, I spent a few nights in a tent, but that was about as wild as it got for us growing up in a family of all girls. He was quite sad one time when I broke the news to him that my very pregnant body just couldn't handle sleeping on the ground and entertaining a toddler in a tent all night. That day, while he was at work, my little buddy and I decided to set up an indoor campsite to surprise Dad when he got home. He may not have been as excited as he would have been if we had really gone camping, but these s'mores bars sure eased his pain. —Elyse

½ cup butter, room temperature	¾ cup graham cracker crumbs
¼ cup brown sugar	1 teaspoon baking powder
½ cup granulated sugar	¼ teaspoon salt
1 large egg	3 king-sized milk chocolate bars (such as Hershey's)
1 teaspoon vanilla	
1⅓ cups all-purpose flour	1½ cups marshmallow crème

Preheat oven to 350 degrees F. Grease an 8x8-inch baking pan.

In a large bowl, cream together butter and sugars until light and fluffy. Beat in egg and vanilla. In a small bowl, whisk together flour, graham cracker crumbs, baking powder, and salt. Add to butter mixture and mix at a low speed until combined.

Divide dough in half and press half of dough evenly on the bottom of the prepared pan. Place chocolate bars over dough (3 king-sized Hershey's bars should fit perfectly side by side, but break the chocolate, if necessary, to get it to fit in a single layer no more than ¼-inch thick). Spread marshmallow crème over chocolate layer. Place remaining dough in a single layer on top of the marshmallow (most easily achieved by flattening the dough into small, flat shingles and laying them together).

Bake 30 to 35 minutes, until lightly browned. Cool completely before cutting into bars.

Makes 16 bars.

DO-IT-YOURSELF RUFFLES AND YARN WREATH

This wreath is so fun to make, and the entire project can be completed in about an hour. Switch up the colors of the yarn and ruffles to match décor for any holiday.

SUPPLIES

- 1 skein (about 165 yards) yarn, any color
- 1 14-inch foam wreath form
- ½ yard felt, any color
- scissors
- ruler
- needle and thread
- hot glue

INSTRUCTIONS

1. **Wrap the wreath.** Place a dot of hot glue on the back of the form. Glue down the end of the yarn and start wrapping tightly. Go around the whole form twice. Use another dot of hot glue to hold down the end when finished. Trim off any leftover yarn.

2. **Cut three strips of felt.** Cut the felt into three 24-inch long strips of varying widths: the first should be 6 inches wide, the second 4.5 inches wide, and the third 2.5 inches wide.

3. **Sew the felt into a ruffle.** Lay the three strips of felt on top of each other with the

When you reach the end of the felt, cinch it as tightly as you want and tie a knot so that it will stay in place.

largest one on the bottom. Using your needle and thread, sew a simple running stitch down the middle.

As you sew, cinch your material so that it begins to ruffle (it is much easier to do this as you go instead of at the end because the felt is so thick).

Keep sewing and cinching as you go.

4. **Attach the ruffle.** Wrap your ruffle around the wreath wherever you want it and glue it securely in place.

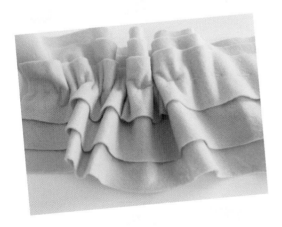

Easy Banana Cream Bars

The secret to this recipe is the Nilla Wafer crust. It perfectly complements the cool, creamy banana filling.

80 Nilla Wafer cookies, crushed (about one 12-ounce box)

½ cup butter, melted

1 (8-ounce) package cream cheese, softened

2 cups powdered sugar

2 (8-ounce) containers nondairy whipped topping, divided

1 (5.1-ounce) package banana cream instant pudding

2 cups milk

3 bananas, sliced

Preheat oven to 350 degrees F. Mix together the crushed cookies and melted butter. Press into a 9x13-inch baking pan. Bake 10 minutes. Let cool.

Beat together cream cheese, powdered sugar, and 1 container whipped topping. Spread on top of cooled cookie crust.

Beat together the banana cream pudding with milk. Let stand 4 to 5 minutes until thickened. Spread on top of cream cheese layer.

Spread sliced bananas on top of pudding, covering the entire pan. Spread the second container of whipped topping on top of the bananas. Refrigerate at least 2 hours before serving. Cut into bars and serve.

Makes 16 to 24 bars.

Easy Bite-Sized Apple Pies

These little pies are perfect if you are short on time but are craving the flavor of a delicious apple pie.

½ cup sugar

2 teaspoons cinnamon

1 (14.1-ounce) package Pillsbury refrigerated pie crust

3 tablespoons melted butter, divided

2 medium tart apples, unpeeled, each cut into 8 wedges

Preheat oven to 425 degrees F. Line a baking sheet with parchment paper.

In a small bowl, combine sugar and cinnamon. Remove 1 tablespoon of the cinnamon sugar and set aside. On a lightly floured surface, unroll the pastry. Brush with 2 tablespoons melted butter. Sprinkle all but the reserved cinnamon sugar over top. Cut each sheet into 8 one-inch strips. Wrap one strip around each apple wedge, placing sugared side of pastry against apple. Place on parchment paper-lined baking sheet. Brush tops with remaining melted butter and sprinkle with reserved cinnamon sugar. Bake 13 to 15 minutes, until pastry is golden brown. Serve warm.

Makes 16 bite-sized pies.

THE ULTIMATE

KID WASH

Don't be intimidated by this seemingly elaborate contraption. You can totally do this! And your kids will love you for it during those dog days of summer. Take the supply list to Lowe's or Home Depot, hand it to one of the sales associates, and they can find all these little pieces for you. Also, have them cut your pipes; if it is a slower day, they will happily do it for you!

SUPPLIES

- 2 (10-foot) ¾-inch PVC pipes, cut according to directions in step 1
- 3 (10-foot) ½-inch PVC pipes, cut according to directions in step 1
- 4 (½-inch) PVC tees
- 4 (¾-inch to ½-inch) threaded PVC side outlet elbows
- 4 (½-inch) male adapters
- 7 (½-inch) end caps
- 1 (½-inch) hose adapter
- primer
- cement drill with ¼-sized drill bit

INSTRUCTIONS

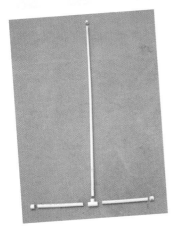

1. **Cut longer pieces.** Cut the long ¾-inch pipes into 2 five-foot pieces and 2 three-foot pieces. Cut the ½-inch pipes into 4 five-foot pieces and 8 one-foot pieces.

2. **Make 3 Ts.** Make 3 of these upside-down T-shapes. For each T, use one ½-inch five-foot pipe, two ½-inch 1-foot pipes, 1 tee, and 2 end caps. Place a male adapter at the top.

3. **Build another T.** Build one more upside-down T, only this time use one end cap and one hose adapter.

3. **Prime and cement.** Prime your pieces and cement them into place.

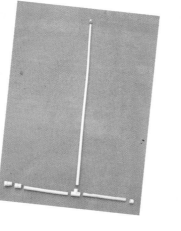

4. **Drill holes.** Drill randomly-placed holes in the four ¾-inch pipes. (2 of these will be 5 feet in length and 2 of them will be 3 feet in length.)

5. **Make a rectangle.** Piece the 4 drilled pipes together with the threaded side outlet elbows to make a rectangle. Holes drilled in the pipes should be angled slightly in (toward the center) to ensure maximum soakability! Prime and cement the rectangle. Let it dry.

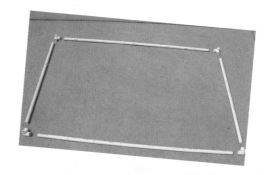

6. **Assemble Ultimate Kid Wash.** Screw the four T-shaped legs into the rectangle top. Plug a hose to the adapter on the bottom. Turn the hose on as high as you can for the strongest water stream.

Easy Strawberry Napoleons

My husband and I took a trip to Disney World one year. While there, we wandered into a little French bakery and decided to try a lovely dessert known as a Napoleon. We made our way back to the same bakery every night for the rest of the trip to get a taste of those beautiful little pastries! Since then, we just can't seem to get enough Napoleons in our life. Thank goodness for this great make-at-home recipe.—Elyse

1   sheet frozen puff pastry

1   (3.4-ounce) package instant vanilla pudding

1   cup milk

1   teaspoon almond extract

1   cup whipped topping (nondairy or real whipped cream)

2   cups stemmed and sliced strawberries

⅓   cup sliced almonds, toasted (optional)

Powdered sugar, for garnish

Preheat oven to 400 degrees F. Thaw folded pastry sheet for 20 minutes. Open sheet and cut along folds to make three equal strips; halve each strip to make six rectangles. Space a couple of inches apart on baking sheet. Bake in center of oven about 15 minutes, until well browned and baked through. Remove to rack to cool.

Meanwhile, whisk pudding mix, milk, and almond extract in a bowl for 2 minutes; fold in whipped topping and blend thoroughly. Cover and refrigerate.

Carefully split each piece of pastry in half, or in thirds, horizontally. Cover bottom halves with almonds, then pudding mixture and sliced strawberries, dividing equally. Cover with pastry tops. Dust with powdered sugar.

Makes 4 3-layer pastries or 6 2-layer pastries.

Mini Oreo Cheesecakes

Cheesecake + Oreos = a match made in heaven! These mini cheesecakes are made in a muffin tin so they are easy to transport to a party and serve to guests. Top each cheesecake with whipped cream and rich hot fudge and no one will be able to resist them!

24 whole Oreo cookies

3 (8-ounce) packages cream cheese, softened

¾ cup sugar

1 teaspoon vanilla

3 eggs

12 Oreo cookies, crushed

Whipped cream

Hot fudge or chocolate syrup

Additional Oreo cookie crumbs for garnish

Preheat oven to 350 degrees F. Place 24 cupcake liners in muffin tins. Set a whole Oreo cookie in the bottom of each liner.

In a large bowl, beat together cream cheese, sugar, and vanilla until very smooth. Add eggs one at a time, mixing until just blended. Gently fold in the crushed Oreo cookies. Spoon cheesecake mixture over each cookie in the liners. Bake 15 to 20 minutes or until the center of each cheesecake is almost set. Cool completely, then refrigerate at least 1 hour (or overnight). Top with a dollop of whipped cream, drizzle with chocolate sauce, and sprinkle crushed Oreo cookies on top.

Makes 24 mini cheesecakes.

Skinny Funfetti Cupcakes

After having a baby, I felt a little depressed when thinking about getting back in shape. Going without dessert makes life so unbearable, so rather than giving it up completely, I decided to try making a dessert I didn't have to feel as guilty about.—Elyse

1 (15.25-ounce) package Pillsbury Funfetti cake mix

1 (12-ounce) can Sprite Zero

1 (8-ounce) container fat-free nondairy whipped topping

1 (1.5-ounce) package vanilla instant pudding

Preheat oven to 350 degrees F. Line 24 cupcake tins with paper liners. In a large bowl, combine dry cake mix and Sprite. Continue to mix until the batter is smooth without any lumps. Pour approximately ¼ cup of batter into every cupcake wrapper. Bake 20 minutes. Let cool.

When cupcakes are completely cooled, use an electric mixer to combine whipped topping and pudding until smooth. Spread over cupcakes.

Makes 2 dozen cupcakes.

Black Forest Cherry Cupcakes

These cupcakes are a twist on an old family favorite. They make the perfect treat for any family party or potluck dinner and are always a big hit! Keep them in the refrigerator until serving—they are so good cold!

- 24 devil's food cupcakes
- 1 (8-ounce) package cream cheese, softened
- 1 cup powdered sugar
- 1 teaspoon vanilla
- 1 (8-ounce) container nondairy whipped topping
- 1 (16-ounce) can cherry pie filling

Prepare 24 devil's food cupcakes according to package directions on boxed cake mix.

While the cupcakes are cooling, beat together cream cheese, powdered sugar, and vanilla in a medium bowl. Fold in whipped topping until well blended. Spread on cooled cupcakes. Top with cherry pie filling. Keep in the fridge until ready to serve.

Makes 24 cupcakes.

Cinnamon Roll Cake

Anything with cinnamon in it has to be good! This cake is easy to assemble and tastes amazing. We've been known to eat it straight out of the oven when it's warm and oh-so-gooey. It has all the flavor of a yummy cinnamon roll without all the work!

3 cups plus 2 tablespoons all-purpose flour, divided	2 teaspoons vanilla
1 cup sugar	4 tablespoons butter, melted
¼ teaspoon salt	1 tablespoon brown sugar
4 teaspoons baking powder	1 cup butter, softened
1 teaspoon cinnamon	1 cup brown sugar
1½ cups milk	1 tablespoon cinnamon
2 eggs	⅔ cup walnuts (optional)
	Glaze (see recipe below)

Preheat oven to 350 degrees F. Grease a 9x13-inch baking dish. Combine 3 cups flour, sugar, salt, baking powder, 1 teaspoon cinnamon, milk, eggs, and vanilla in the bowl of a stand mixer and mix on medium speed. Once well combined, slowly stir in the 4 tablespoons melted butter. Pour batter into prepared pan and sprinkle on 1 tablespoon brown sugar over the top of the cake; set aside.

In a large bowl, mix softened butter, brown sugar, 2 tablespoons flour, cinnamon, and nuts until well combined. Drop evenly over cake batter by the tablespoon and use a knife to swirl through the cake, making a marble design. Bake 25 to 30 minutes or until a toothpick comes out nearly clean from center. Drizzle Glaze over warm cake. Serve warm or at room temperature.

GLAZE

2 cups powdered sugar	1 teaspoon vanilla
5 tablespoons milk	

Whisk powdered sugar, milk, and vanilla in a large bowl until smooth.

Pineapple Orange Cake

This cake is light, fruity, and delicious in the hot summer months. It is perfect to take to a potluck or BBQ and very simple to make.

◇◇

1 (15.25-ounce) package yellow cake mix

1 (11-ounce) can mandarin oranges, undrained

4 egg whites

½ cup unsweetened applesauce

1 (20-ounce) can crushed pineapple, undrained

1 (3.5-ounce) package vanilla instant pudding mix

1 (8-ounce) container reduced-fat nondairy whipped topping

Preheat oven to 350 degrees F. Coat a 9x13-inch baking dish with nonstick cooking spray.

In a large bowl, beat together cake mix, oranges, egg whites, and applesauce on low speed for 2 minutes. Pour into prepared baking dish and bake 25 to 30 minutes, or until a toothpick inserted near the center comes out clean. Cool on a wire rack.

In a medium bowl, combine pineapple and pudding mix. Fold in whipped topping just until blended. Spread over cake. Refrigerate at least 1 hour before serving. Garnish with sliced oranges, if desired.

Makes 12 to 16 servings.

Peach Dump Cake

This cake takes only a few minutes to assemble and tastes great with a scoop of vanilla ice cream on top.

2 (16-ounce) cans peaches in heavy syrup

1 (15.25-ounce) package yellow cake mix

½ cup butter

½ teaspoon cinnamon, or to taste

Preheat oven to 375 degrees F. Pour peaches into the bottom of a 9x13-inch baking pan. Cover with the dry cake mix and press down firmly. Cut butter into small pieces and place on top of cake mix. Sprinkle top with cinnamon. Bake for 45 minutes.

Makes 10 to 12 servings.

Baked Cinnamon Sugar Churros

This baked version of a churro turns out amazing, crunchy, cinnamon goodness in 15 minutes flat.

1 sheet frozen pastry puff, thawed

½ cup sugar

2 teaspoons cinnamon

¼ cup butter, melted

Preheat oven to 450 degrees F. Line a baking sheet with parchment paper and grease lightly. Unfold and cut puff pastry sheet in half lengthwise. Cut each half crosswise into 1-inch-wide strips. Place strips on parchment paper and bake 8 to 10 minutes or until golden brown. Meanwhile, combine sugar and cinnamon. Remove pastries from oven and dip in butter, then roll in cinnamon-sugar mixture. Let stand on a wire rack 5 minutes or until dry.

Makes 18 churros.

Chubby Hubby Buckeye Truffles

Whether it's for your hubby, kids, or the neighbors, these truffles are the perfect combination of peanut butter, chocolate, and pretzel to please almost anyone. The sweet and salty flavors combine to make these tempting truffles one delicious treat!

1½ cups pretzel pieces	3 tablespoons powdered sugar
½ cup creamy peanut butter	1 cup milk or semisweet chocolate chips
1 tablespoon unsalted butter, room temperature	1 tablespoon shortening
2 tablespoons light brown sugar	Additional peanut butter, melted, for garnish
Pinch of salt	Additional pretzel pieces, for garnish

Line a baking sheet with parchment paper or waxed paper. Put the pretzel pieces into a resealable gallon-sized plastic bag and crush into very small bits (a rolling pin works great for this).

In a small bowl, combine peanut butter, butter, brown sugar, and salt. Stir until all of the ingredients are completely blended and smooth. Add pretzel bits to the peanut butter mixture and mix thoroughly. Add powdered sugar and mix until completely combined.

Shape dough into 1-inch balls and place on prepared baking sheet. Place baking sheet in refrigerator and chill for at least 30 minutes.

When ready to dip the truffles, microwave the chocolate chips and shortening together in a small bowl at 50 percent power in 30-second increments, stirring after each, until completely melted and smooth.

Working one at a time, dip one peanut butter ball into the melted chocolate and use a fork to roll it around, ensuring that it is completely coated with chocolate. Let any excess chocolate drip off and place back on the waxed paper. Repeat until each peanut butter ball has been dipped.

Return the baking sheet to the refrigerator and chill for at least 30 minutes. Garnish with a drizzle of melted peanut butter and crushed pretzels, if desired. Store in an airtight container in the refrigerator.

Makes about 18 truffles.

$6

WIRE HANGER
CHRISTMAS
ORNAMENT
WREATH

This wreath takes about 30 minutes to make, doesn't require a wreath form—just a wire hanger—and costs only $6 if you buy your ornaments at a dollar store, but you'd never guess any of that by looking at the finished product!

SUPPLIES

- 1 wire hanger
- 80 ornaments (varied sizes if desired)
- pliers
- hot glue gun
- 6 to 9 feet wired ribbon (about 2 inches wide) with the same print on both sides
- thin craft wire

INSTRUCTIONS

1. **Make a wreath form.** Bend the wire hanger into a circle and then use pliers to untwist the wire at the top.

2. **String on the ornaments.** One by one, string on the ornaments. If using different sizes, colors, or textures, arrange to suit your tastes. Make sure to push your ornaments together as close as you can so that the wire doesn't show through. Think of it as a puzzle and try to put each ornament at a different angle around the

hanger. The following pictures show varying stages of the stringing process to give you an idea of how the wreath will come together.

Occasionally you might have an ornament that pops off its hook. If this happens, apply a drop of hot glue to secure it.

3. **Twist the hanger together.** Once all the ornaments are strung and placed how you like them, use the pliers to twist the hanger back together.

4. **Hide the hanger's hook**. Wrap a portion of the wired ribbon around the wreath at the hanger's hook 2 times so that the hook is completely hidden. Secure the ribbon at the back with hot glue.

5. **Make a bow.** Make a 6- to 8-inch loop on one end of the ribbon. If you want tails for your bow, leave a few inches at the end of the ribbon and then make the first loop.

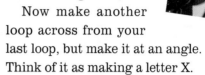

Holding the loop in the middle, make another loop directly across from the first (so if you looked at this on its side, it would look like a figure 8.)

Now make another loop across from your last loop, but make it at an angle. Think of it as making a letter X.

Make another loop across from your last one to finish your letter X.

You can stop here or you can add 1 more loop—just make another X. When you are finished with the loops, scrunch the loops in the middle with your fingers nice and tight.

Wrap some wire around the middle of the bow—the tighter, the better!

Trim your tails to the length you want them and clean up the ends a little bit.

To cover up the wire in the middle of the bow, take a piece of ribbon that is about 6 inches long and tie a knot in the middle of it.

Glue that knot down in the middle of the bow using hot glue.

Wrap the ends back behind the bow, glue them down, and trim them.

6. **Attach the bow.** Use hot glue to attach the bow near the covered hanger hook.

No-Bake Thin Mint Cookie Truffles

These little balls of goodness are amazing, especially if you love a mint and chocolate combo. Best part about them: no baking required and only 4 ingredients needed!

1 (9-ounce) package Girl Scout Thin Mint Cookies or Keebler Grasshopper cookies

4 ounces cream cheese, softened

1 (12-ounce) bag Guittard Green Mint Chips

Almond bark or semisweet chocolate, melted

Line a baking sheet with parchment paper. In a food processor, pulse the Thin Mints a few times, and then blend them down until they are just crumbs. If you don't have a food processor, place the cookies in a resealable gallon-sized plastic bag and pound them with a hammer or rolling pin until you have a lot of fine crumbs. Mix the cream cheese and cookie crumbs together in a bowl until combined well. Roll the mixture into 1-inch balls and place them on prepared baking sheet. Place the baking sheet in the fridge for about 30 minutes. Once the truffles have been in the fridge for a while, melt the green mint chips in a microwave-safe bowl in the microwave. Heat the chips in 30-second increments at 50 percent power, stirring between each increment. Repeat until the chips are all melted.

Roll each ball in the melted chips with two forks until it is all covered. Then, using the two forks, carefully pick up the truffle and allow the excess mint chocolate to run off before placing it back on the parchment paper. Repeat with all the truffles.

Refrigerate for a couple of minutes or until the mint chocolate is hardened. Drizzle with melted almond bark or semisweet chocolate and return briefly to refrigerator to set.

Makes about 18 truffles.

Funfetti Cake Batter Buddies

Do you have 10 minutes? If so, run into the kitchen and throw this amazing little snack together! It's crazy addicting, so you might want to double the batch.

10 ounces (5 squares) vanilla-flavored almond bark

1 teaspoon shortening

5 cups Chex cereal

1½ cups Funfetti cake mix

½ cup powdered sugar

Melt almond bark according to the package directions, adding vegetable shortening to thin.

Pour the cereal into a large bowl and drizzle the melted almond bark over the cereal. Mix gently with a large spoon or spatula.

Pour the cake mix and powdered sugar onto the cereal and mix gently with a large spoon until all the cereal is evenly coated.

Makes about 6 cups snack mix.

INDEX